THE JESUS
CODE

Also by John Randolph Price

Books

The Abundance Book
*Angel Energy
*The Angels Within Us
Empowerment
*Living a Life of Joy
The Love Book
The Meditation Book
Practical Spirituality
A Spiritual Philosophy for the New World
The Success Book
The Superbeings
The Wellness Book
With Wings As Eagles
The Workbook for Self-Mastery

Selected Audiocassettes

The 40-Day Prosperity Plan
A Journey into the Fourth Dimension
The Manifestation Process
Prayer, Principles & Power

Check your bookstore for the books and audios above. All items
except those with asterisks can be ordered through Hay House:
800-654-5126 • 800-650-5115 (fax)

Please visit the Hay House Website at: **www.hayhouse.com**

THE JESUS CODE

John Randolph Price

Hay House, Inc.
Carlsbad, California • Sydney, Australia

Published and distributed in the United States by: Hay House, Inc.,
P.O. Box 5100, Carlsbad, CA 92018-5100
(800) 654-5126 • (800) 650-5115 (fax)

Editorial: Jill Kramer   *Design:* Jenny Richards

Library of Congress Cataloging-in-Publication Data

Price, John Randolph.
     The Jesus code / John Randolph Price.
          p.   cm.
     Includes bibliographical references.
     ISBN 1-56170-671-X (tradepaper)
      1. Spiritual life—Christianity—Miscellanea.   2. Jesus Christ—
New Thought interpretations.   I. Title.
BV4509.5.P735   2000
299'.93—dc21   99-15923
                                   CIP

ISBN: 1-56170-671-X

03 02 01 00   5 4 3 2
1st printing, February 2000
2nd printing, August 2000

Printed in Canada

Dedicated to the Path Walkers

THE GOLDEN ARROW

May the most holy, most sacred, most adorable, most incomprehensible and ineffable Name of God be forever praised, blessed, loved, adored and glorified in Heaven, on earth, and under the earth, by all the creatures of God, and by the Sacred Heart of Our Lord Jesus Christ, in the Most Holy Sacrament of the Altar. Amen.

(Dictated by Our Lord to Sr. Marie of St. Peter)

Eternal Father, I offer Thee the adorable Face of Thy Beloved Son for the honor and glory of Thy Name, for the conversion of sinners and the salvation of the dying.

"Oh Jesus, through the merits of your Holy Face, have pity on us, and on the whole world".
(Three times).

...ENTS

APPENDIX

INTRODUCTION

On the night of January 1, 1998, I had an experience that led to the discovery of the Jesus Code. The word *code* comes from the Latin *Codex,* meaning "a book of laws or principles"— in this case representing particular steps to a deeper awareness, understanding, and knowledge of our true nature.

It all began in a dream. I was seated in front of my computer trying to bring up a master document on cosmic consciousness. Suddenly two large words filled the screen: ACCESS DENIED. I stared at the screen wondering what to do next. Then across the bottom appeared these words in red letters: *See Jesus for the code.*

I woke up with a feeling best described as startled and excited—surprised at being denied admittance to higher understanding, yet greatly inspired to follow the instructions given. I must admit that for most of my early adult life, my relationship with Jesus was rather impersonal—primarily because of the traditional church's portrayal of him as a somber, sorrowful, sacrificial martyr, with suffering and persecution the necessary elements of discipleship. But the remnants of this attitude left me when I began doing research in the late 1970s for my first book, *The Superbeings*, so I was eager to follow the assignment.

Prayerful, listening meditations produced bits and pieces of information, but it was not until I took a break from the project one day and went for a walk in the woods with my dogs that the first part of the Code was given. I was enjoying the cool, fresh air when suddenly I heard the message—not audible words, but a clear voice in my mind. It said:

> *Be me . . . everyone is the Son of God, the Christ, and I am your brother in the family of God. Identify as me, as what I represent, not only as the Christ, but as individual being with body, personality, mind, feelings, and spirit as one. Be me! Be the whole person I represent. The Code is to believe . . . I AM AS JESUS.*

There was more, but let's pause here. First, do not be turned off by the term *Christ*. It is pre-Christian and came from Plato's *Christos*, meaning "the True Self of everyone." Second, for centuries our attention has been directed either to the Christian Jesus as the only God-in-the-flesh, the only Begotten, the one Lord and Savior of mankind—or as God's perfect idea of individual being in expression, the great Example of what we all may someday become. The former has been redefined in accordance with Jesus' true mission and purpose by the enlightened ones for 2,000 years, and the latter considered for all practical purposes a near-impossible goal to reach in life.

Mystical writings have also emphasized that we are not a body, that the ego of personality must be dissolved, and that we must die daily to our personal sense. But now, at least for me, a new perspective was given. The communication of the Code continued:

You have a physical body just as I did, so do not attempt to sacrifice it on the altar of spirituality. Use the body proudly, love it, and care for it as a visible expression of yourself.

You are consciousness; therefore, you have a personality, as I do, which is an expression of your uniqueness. Do not deny or condemn it, or the world will lose a particular flavor in the great miscellany of life.

You have a mind with which to think. Do not lose it through atrophy in an attempt to become more spiritual in non-thought. The mind that was in Christ Jesus is every mind; there is no mortal or carnal mind.

You have feelings, as I do, otherwise you would be an automaton. Do not suppress them. Truly express your love and joy, your tenderness and compassion. If a false emotion stirs you from past conditioning, transmute it through harmlessness.

You are the Spirit of God, which I am and everyone is. The one Life, your Life, as the perfection of God must forever remain so. Unite with the Truth of me to discover your own Reality.

By identifying as me, as Representative Being, you and others will recognize your completeness, for God does not exist as separate Being. In Truth there is nothing to overcome, nothing to redeem, nothing to heal . . . only beliefs to the contrary to be corrected.

Do I believe that this communication came directly from Jesus? We share the universal Christ Consciousness individually as our divine Selfhood, so to receive specific messages from "this mind which was in Christ Jesus" is quite common for those on the spiritual path—including many who are reading this book. And the Jesus-the-man energy—ever available to us in this planetary force field when we are receptive to it—also contributes a certain tone and flavor from the vantage point of someone who has walked the earth with body and personality. So yes, I do believe that the words, which were interpreted through the filter of my consciousness, came from the whole person of Jesus.

My understanding is that the communication represents a call for all of us to awaken and go forth into the world as spiritual beings temporarily clothed in physical form and expressing as a unique personality, that we are not to deny any part of us. Rather, we are to look at the Jesus Model for our completeness—spiritually, mentally, emotionally, and physically.

Again, do not let the Jesus Code signal a return to the negative feelings of orthodox religion and the church concept of Jesus with all its judgments, sin, sacrifice, blood-shedding, and vicarious death. The Code moves beyond that false teaching and emphasizes that Jesus is a joyful and loving brother who is showing us that a physical life with thoughts and feelings conveying a personality on earth is no less spiritual than the invisible masters who dwell in other dimensions.

In essence, he is saying, "I was physical, I had a personality, I used my mind, and I expressed my feelings—all in unison as the Spirit of God, which all of you are. So stand strong as a complete person, apologizing not for wearing a coat of skin or for being the sum-total of your experiences. The world needs you as you are, and your false beliefs will be corrected as you take *all of you* into spiritual consciousness."

Over a period of several weeks following the initial Code input, specific steps to spiritual or higher consciousness came into my mind, some of which I had already contemplated as separate issues or principles. But now, everything began to come together as a ladder to climb to a new dimension of Reality where the illusions of sickness, scarcity, and discord are shattered; and a world of wholeness, abundance, and right relations is revealed. I show the lesson received at the beginning of each chapter, and then add my own interpretation, relative personal experiences, and/or meditations for greater understanding.

I later looked at *JESUS The Son of Man*[1] by Kahlil Gibran, and certain passages leaped out at me, as though to document what was said in the Code. Those who knew him talked about the rhythm of his step and the movement of his body, his playfulness and laughter, his thoughtful contemplations, his feelings of love and joy, and his recognition of the truth of everyone. He represented the complete person, and he simply asks that we view that completeness as our very own—*I am as Jesus*, not to come, but now.

Gibran also shared the views of those who were not Jesus' friends. They called him a magician, drunkard, rabble-rouser, corrupter, woman-seeker, friend of prostitutes, and lawbreaker. This only added another dimension to the Code. It made me realize even more that Jesus was no different from us, in that our personality—the identity we present to the world—may not be liked by everyone. As long as we're playing a role on the world stage—as everyone on the planet is—people are going to see us from contrasting perspectives, and that's all right. Let's just be true to ourselves, put away our defenses, and get on with the work of being the whole person we are—an "individual being with body, personality, mind, feelings, and spirit as one."

Let's accept the basic premise of the Code—*I am as Jesus*—and keep that truth etched firmly in mind as we climb the steps of the spiritual ladder to a new reality of life and living.

It is time.

LESSON 1

Begin Anew

✛ ✛ ✛

*It is not what you do not know that is retarding
your progress on the path, but what you think you
know. Knowledge of truth filled with strains of error
thoughts produces discordance, which is projected
in the external world as disharmonies of life, yet one
cannot be given up without the other. To begin anew,
you must empty the vessel of perceptions deemed
trustworthy, and carried with them will be the
impurities of false beliefs. Give up the greater
to remove the lesser.*

✛ ✛ ✛

This appears to be a difficult assignment, but it can be accomplished by our willingness to learn from the vantage point of a clean slate. When we give up all the truth we seem to know, we are literally emptying consciousness momentarily in preparation for a greater inflow. And returning to our minds may be the basic spiritual understanding gained through our studies and meditation, but it will be less cluttered, the key points greatly enhanced.

Since we began our journey in remembering our truth of being, we have read many books, listened to a variety of tapes, attended workshops on different ways to storm the gates of the kingdom, and have prayed, meditated, affirmed, and decreed—all of which have led us to where we are now. In my case, the Spirit within has been telling me for years to *simplify, simplify, simplify*—that too much "knowledge" was counterproductive to locking in to a firm position in spiritual consciousness. And I was reminded that in ancient times, the students in the Mystery Schools were told to leave their perceived enlightenment, their comprehension of what constituted reality, outside the door, and they were then directed to ponder single threads of truth until they were realized in consciousness.

They were learning to be co-creators with their Divine Consciousness by seeking a change in mind and heart, in the way they viewed themselves and God. Then, with a deeper spiritual awareness combined with a heightened image of their optimal goals in life, they went forth to create the greatest masterpieces in art, literature, music, and architecture that the world had ever known. They were also instruments of peace—circles of harmony that healed and brought order through the ripple effect.

In this new beginning, let's give up everything we think we know and accept the new inflow from Spirit.

I am ready and willing to give up everything I think I know, including all false beliefs, in exchange for fresh insights into the verities of life.

As I release it all, I feel the energy of my entire force field—every thought and belief, all convictions— being lifted up, flowing upward into the light to be transmuted. I see and feel this happening now.

As the last vestige rises out of the shadows, I can truly say . . . I know nothing. I know nothing! All thoughts and beliefs have been given up to be purified.

My consciousness is clear and clean, free, a vacuum, ready now for a new infilling. I am ready.

I am now receiving the new inflow of divine thoughts and perfect patterns from Spirit. I feel the Mind of spiritual understanding and divine wisdom entering the crown above my head and flowing downward, filling, filling, filling. I do not try to think. I let the one Mind think for me.

I rest in the Silence.

Now we are ready to progress through the steps—to see and know in the same way that Spirit, our God-Self, sees and knows. And for our beginning thread of Truth that will allow us safe passage into the eternal NOWS of glorious living, let's contemplate this one:

I do not dwell in the past, for it does not exist, and neither do any stains remain from the yesterdays of life. I have received a fresh infilling from Spirit, and all past sorrows and compulsive fears have been removed. I am now free to climb the ladder to full and complete spiritual consciousness.

I begin anew.

LESSON 2

Know God Aright

*God Transcendent, greater than all of creation,
appears as God Immanent, pervading all creation.
The Unknown Pure Being beholds Itself as Spirit and
Truth, and the great Light of Love and Life emerges
as Intimate Spirit. This is Universal Selfhood, not a
separate creation or reflection, but the Presence of
God being the individual Purpose in and as all.*

*God is; and outside of God, nothing exists,
for all is God and God is Love.*

I believe that it is our misunderstanding of God that has thrown the entire world into turmoil for thousands of years. In many religions, it was as though God was created in the human image—in the image of the lower nature—and this human concept of God was pronounced both good and evil and given dominion over every living thing. And as the ancient texts tell us, "Great fear spread across the land."

In the Babylonian creation stories, the gods, clothed in terror and filled with anger, created all manner of evil to destroy the seed of humankind. And in Egypt, the gods sought to make all people their slaves and violently established ways of worship. Then we have Jehovah of the Old Testament who promised blood throughout the land, conjured up the ten plagues, and "smote all the firstborn." God, created in the image of man, was cruel, persecuting, and vengeful. And we can see that such a teaching could certainly produce dysfunctional lives and become a mental health hazard.

It has been taught by the illumined ones for eons that God is the Primal Power of Will-for-Good, Love, Life, and Creative Intelligence—and that this is a benevolent universe where nothing but beauty and goodness exist. How did they know this? Through faith? Perhaps so in the distant past when God was referred to as "The One About Whom Naught May Be Said." This was God Transcendent, the Great Unknown, only a nebulous Presence to even the highest initiate. But in time, the ancient mystics began to understand the nature of God by *experiencing* God Immanent as their Intimate Spirit, as the very Life of their being. They realized God dwelling within as omniscient Love, omnipotent Principle, and omnipresent Spirit—one Presence, one Mind, one Power—closer than breathing.

God *IS*; and outside of God, nothing exists, which means that we can experience the Reality of ourselves because *all is God*. The fullness of the Godhead is totally embodied in the indwelling, interpenetrating, overshadowing Divine Consciousness of each individual, the holy *I*, which is our true and only nature.

We can know God because "I and my Consciousness are one"—meaning that our mind of awareness (the soul faculty) and That which we are aware of (Spirit) are one. "All that my Consciousness is, I AM"—all that I recognize within, I AM. Jesus referred to this Infinite Cause as the Father, the fathering (creating) Spirit within, the Known God. Paul called It the Christ in you. Whatever labels we use, let's remember that there is no place where God leaves off and something else comes forth. God *individualizes* as our true and only Self. All is God.

"The God of Pythagoras (the first and most famous philosopher) was the *Monad*, or the One that is Everything. He described God as the Supreme Mind distributed throughout all parts of the universe—the Cause of all things, the Intelligence of all things, and the Power within all things."[1]

In the 13th century, Saint Thomas Aquinas declared that "HE WHO IS" is the most proper name for God. Ralph Waldo Emerson spoke of the *Is* dwelling within and *as* each individual, shining through as Will to pronounce all things good. He wrote, "The simplest person who in his integrity worships God, becomes God."[2]

And according to Alice A. Bailey, the Tibetan Master Djwhal Khul said that "the Life of God, His energy, and vitality, are found in every manifested atom; His essence indwells all forms."[3]

In this second step of our new beginning, let's dismiss all concepts and images of God as an entity separate and apart from us, or as a demander of justice and punishment, a jealous master, an angry ruler, or as one who must be petitioned for gifts, favors, and divine doles. God is absolute goodness, total givingness, does not know the concept of sin or punishment, has created a universe of beauty for Itself, and has expressed as our individual Divine Consciousness—our kingdom of peace and plenty where life is to be enjoyed to the fullest.

Think on these thoughts:

God IS. God is the one universal Presence and Power, the Cosmic Heart of Love, expressing as all that is good, true, and beautiful in life. I am that Expression.

I and the Spirit of God are one and the same. I am God being me, and God loves Itself as me.

I AM.

I AM conscious.

I AM consciously aware.

I AM consciously aware of the presence of God.

I AM consciously aware of the presence of God I AM.

I AM consciously aware of the presence of God I AM as me.

I now listen and hear the Voice of Truth speak from the stillness within.

LESSON 3

Understand the Nature of Soul

*And the I, the Selfhood of God as Intimate Spirit,
contemplated Itself, and from the contemplation
came forth an Awareness of Itself: Sparks from the
Universal Flame in near-infinite individual units
of Self-awareness, Souls, yet undivided and
containing the Whole.*

We do not have a separate mind from Mind. The universal *I-Spirit* in Self-contemplation whirled out, so to speak, fields of consciousness, souls, units of Its own Self-awareness, and remained with that Awareness as the Reality of Being. Ageless Wisdom tells us that "there are sixty thousand million units of consciousness"[1] considering both sides of the veil.

For greater understanding of this concept, think of your conscious mind as an individual soul. Now see this unit of Self-awareness as a ring of light in an infinite sea of light. The Spirit, the *I*, changes Its vibration around the ring and sounds a cosmic note directly related to the soul, your particular consciousness. The Ancients described this configuration of the outer and inner rings together (Spirit and soul as one) as "egg shaped" and referred to it as an "ovum." In a Gnostic tract written in the first century, Jesus' disciples reveal, "We are next given a diagram (by Jesus). . . . The diagram is like an egg, with a smaller egg or nucleus within it. . . ."[2]

The *I-Spirit-Self* individualizes Its Consciousness as a particular energy field while It remains universal. Each one of us is the *I*, omnipresent yet individual, a particularization of *I*. The *I* is our Reality, our Self. If you could step back and look at your Self, you would see a blazing light in, around, and through you—a radiant auric field of infinite intelligence, power, wisdom, and love—universal and fully present at the point where you are. You are that Light!

What we consider as our personal consciousness is our Self in focused expression as Self-awareness. We are not a mortal or carnal mind. Those words signify only a pocket of false belief. We are centers of awareness of *Spirit-I*, not separate from the *I*, but the *I* beholding Itself from a different vibration of Mind. The role or function of the soul is to be consciously aware of Divine Reality, think thoughts of Truth, and envision a world of perfection. The *I-Self* then manifests form and experience in, through, and *as* that consciousness. Creation is constant; it never ceases.

Jesus spoke of this when he said, referring to his awareness-of-Consciousness-within, "I can of mine own self do nothing." (Jn 5:30) And "If I bear witness of myself, my witness is not true." (Jn 5:31) But later, speaking as the Divine *I*—the Self of everyone—he said, "I am the way, and the truth, and the life." (Jn 14:16) And "He who has seen me has seen the Father (Divine Consciousness at work)." (Jn 14:9)

In the Pistis Sophia Treatise of the Gnostics, Jesus says: "Do ye still not know and are ye ignorant? Know ye not and do ye not understand that ye are all Angels, all Archangels, Gods and Lords, all Rulers, all the great Invisibles, all those of the Midst, those of every region of them that are on the Right, all the Great Ones of the emanations of the Light with all their glory. . . ."[3]

Another point we should consider here: The Spirit of God is the creative principle of the universe, and that same Spirit is the Cause at work in and through our mind and feeling nature. Creation of a high order is at work when we are aware, understand, and know the Presence within—our Holy Self—and see with our imaging faculty the fullness of life more abundant. (We see the truth and not a lie.) Then the Self lives as us, and a time will come when the awareness and the Personality of the *I* are one and the same, as shown in the Jesus example.

There is not me and thee, there is only Me. Because repetition is so important for understanding, let's look again at our divine constitution. First, I am, we are, the Spirit-Self of God embodying the fullness of the Godhead. Ponder this. Almighty God, the Primal Power, the Eternal IS, the First Principle, dwells within us. When we see and feel the Presence within, it is not just our higher nature we are sensing, but the Allness of God—Father, Mother, Spirit-Self as One.

The second aspect of our being is the soul of Self-awareness, our personality, called by the Ancients the "Light of the Lord." It is the transmitter of substance to create form and experience, the medium for the expression of Spirit, and the mind of personal identification. So the whole of us is an "individual being with body, personality, mind, feelings, and spirit as one." *I am as Jesus.*

What about the ego? It is nothing but a thought-form of fear—the seat of all false beliefs—that we created in our minds as we began to sense a separation from our true nature. It has no reality, and its illusionary grip is being lessened with each step we take in the light.

A Meditation

Who am I? I ask the question and listen to the voice deep within.

I am the only Presence there is, infinite, omnipresent. I am your Self, the only Self there is. There is no other.

But I feel there are two of us, a me and a You, a lower and higher mind, a helpless creature and a Divine Master.

A wave cannot be separated from the ocean, a ray from the sun. There is only Me, universal and individual. Return to that glory that was once ours—one Mind, one Presence, one Power. I am your Spirit; you are the awareness of Myself through which I function to reveal fulfillment in every area of life.

I am now aware of the I mighty in the midst of me, my one Self expressing as perfect life and perfect world.

I renounce the false belief that I am a human being, and accept the truth that I am pure Spirit expressing as soul and body. God is my only Being, my only Existence.

I am not a human mind, for there is only one Mind— God-Mind—and God did not create anything opposite of Itself.

I am conscious of my only Self, the Truth of my Being. I am aware of Me, the only One, and through this awareness of my Self, the kingdom flows into perfect form and experience.

I am as Jesus—physically, mentally, emotionally, and spiritually. I am a complete being!

LESSON 4

Understand Immortality

There was no birth until death became manifest, yet you were never born and cannot die. Dismiss all such fearful ideas from mind, and be free to live fully now. You are an immortal being of one mind, which to personal sense may appear limited, but is not; and one Body that appears substantial, but is not.

In the early stages of individual life on the planet, there was no necessity for reproduction, and what we know today as death did not exist. We took on form at will, and then through an activity of mind, the electromagnetic force could be altered and the atomic structure rearranged so that the form of the body could literally disappear. We could come and go from one plane to another whenever we so desired.

This change-of-force is not unknown today. Phenomenalist literature is filled with stories of people disappearing into thin air, slowly dematerializing before witnesses, and inexplicably vanishing. There is also the case of Iceland native Indridi Indridason. "In 1905 several of Iceland's leading scientists decided to investigate the paranormal and chose Indridason as one of their subjects . . . sometimes while he was deep in trance, different parts of his body would completely dematerialize. As the astonished scientists watched, an arm or a hand would fade out of existence, only to rematerialize before he was awakened."[1]

Author-historian William Bramley suggests, "Our physical perceptions do not detect the almost illusionary nature of matter because the physical senses are constructed to accept the illusion of solidity caused by the extremely rapid motion of atomic particles. . . . If we could see matter for what it truly was, we would see the most solid object as a piece of whispy fluff."[2] Obviously Indridason did not fully accept the illusion of solidity, at least not while in a meditative state.

In time, we collectively lost not only the ability to dematerialize, but also the knowledge to take on form. Our only alternative in returning to our natural abode was through body elimination. Thus, in ancient Lemuria, the first disease was conceived, which the Wisdom Teachings say was "the great liberator." It was also the beginning of body production through the fusion of cells to provide an entrance for souls to enter the so-called material world. As my wife, Jan, was told in meditation, the imperfection of the physical form began only after we started manufacturing them through the birthing process, which was not a part of the universal scheme of things. Remember, the body is a reflection of consciousness; it takes on both the positive and misqualified energies of the incarnating entity.

Even so, the truth is that we were never born and cannot die. A physical body can be reproduced through the union of male and female cells, and we should value it as our vehicle for use on this plane and repair it as necessary through an elevation of consciousness, which we will discuss later. But we are not that body. If you have ever had an out-of-body or near-death experience, you know that. Our real bodies are pure light, sculptured energy.

And death? It is nothing more than the elimination of the physical system and gaining our freedom from the perceived matter trap, with continuity of life from one realm to another.

The Jesus Example: *Did* he die on the cross? *Could* he? In the Nag Hammadi texts, considered older than the New Testament, the *Apocalypse of Peter* says:

> What am I seeing, O Lord? Is it really you whom they take? And are you holding on to me? And are they hammering the feet and hands of another? Who is the one above the cross, who is glad and laughing? The Savior said to me, "He whom you saw being glad and laughing above the cross is the Living Jesus. But he into whose hands and feet they are driving the nails is his fleshly part, which is the substitute."[3]

Perhaps this was written to emphasize the fact that Jesus had complete control of the situation and did not die on the cross. This was later supported by St. Irenaeus, Bishop of Lyons, who wrote in *Against Heresies* in A.D. 180 that "upon the authority of the Apostles themselves, Jesus lived to old age."

Other evidence tells us that Jesus could not die on the cross because he was a spiritual being, as we are. The *Acts of John*— one of the most famous gnostic texts—explains that Jesus was not a human being at all; instead, he was a spiritual being who adapted himself to human perception. In this work, John is quoted as saying: "I will tell you another glory, brethren; sometimes when I meant to touch him I encountered a material, solid body; but at other times again when I felt him, his substance was immaterial and incorporeal . . . as if it did not exist at all." John adds that he checked carefully for footprints, but Jesus never left any—nor did he ever blink his eyes.[4]

Whether Jesus did not, or could not, die misses the meaning of the crucifixion drama. On the cross, Jesus demonstrated that death is not real, and he proved it with the resurrection. With his realization of the Divine *I*, he had total mastery of the body and the power to heal it instantly, and later to dematerialize it when it was time to leave this plane. And what he did, we can do. Remember the Code: "Be me!" *I am as Jesus.*

Jesus was fully conscious of everything that happened on the cross—and when he removed himself from the physical body, he was able to release the most potent and form-changing energy to enter the earth plane up to that time. The true Identity-Atom in everyone on the planet was activated, thus liberating the *Christos* in all who would follow the Light. Returning once again to his healed body, he showed us our immortality and remained with us to teach fearlessness, wholeness, and unconditional love. Whether he stayed on earth until "old age" is not important, for he is with us now in spirit, united with us in and as the Whole Person we are.

Thought for the day:

> *I am a spiritual being and have adapted myself to the energy of the earth plane, yet I was never born and I shall never die, for God's life is my life, immortal, eternal, forever.*

L E S S O N 5

Dedicate Yourself to the Spiritual Life

There is no higher endeavor than the aspiration to live the spiritual life, for that is your natural state.

All is Spirit, spiritual Mind; there is no other Selfhood, no Presence but the One, yet the Truth may be hidden in a maze of false beliefs. Through commitment to the Light of Reality, misperceptions will be corrected and illumination inevitable.

The aspiration to live the spiritual life, in the realm of Cause, is the highest endeavor because it is a part of the natural process, while ego-centered living is *un*-natural—a desertion of all that is good, true, and beautiful in life to forage for ourselves in the world of effects.

The decision-for-God must be unyielding; the determination to live in and as the only Self must be total. And while this may seem to be a near-impossible task because of our identification with the physical world, the fact that it is our highest aspiration in life will draw forth the very power of Spirit to reinforce the commitment—hour by hour, day by day, as necessary.

When I first began to swim in the spiritual waters, my one thought was how to make certain changes in my life to bring about a more fulfilling career opportunity, a larger income, and a lifestyle more in keeping with my imagination. Nothing wrong with that if it's done the right way. You see, Spirit wants us to have all the material benefits of a life more abundant in every aspect. The will of God in action through the only Selfhood is the law of total and complete fulfillment, with a peaceful mind and a joyful heart as the foundation stones. When the manifestation is from a deep awareness of Spirit as both the Presence and the Law—with the thoughts of our Truth of Being registered in consciousness—we move from on-and-off-again "spurts" of abundance to a continuous all-sufficiency; from physical health to spiritual wholeness; from an ego-oriented job to true place success. On the other hand, demonstrations from a *fearful* ego-effect consciousness will not only bring both light and darkness, but that which is considered "good" will not offer lasting satisfaction.

Now exactly what does it mean to live the spiritual life? It doesn't mean that we have to give up anything in the material world. No, while we may not be *of* this world, we're certainly *in* it, so let's make our experience here the greatest and grandest possible, which can only be done with the acknowledgment of our only Self as the mind, law, and activity of our being.

"All is Spirit, spiritual Mind; there is no other Selfhood, no Presence but the One." Our commitment to living the spiritual life must begin by recognizing the one power, the power within, and giving no power to the effects in the outer world. There must be a giving up of the old ways of thinking, with total reliance on the Presence within for everything. It is keeping our mind focused on our God-Self, the only Self, with intense love and gratitude. And *"misperceptions will be corrected and illumination will be*

inevitable." It is keeping our hands off this world and letting the hands of God show us the Reality behind the illusion of scarcity and limitation. It is a total abandonment to the will of God.

> *"In every aspect of the day Jesus was aware of the Father. He beheld Him in the clouds and in the shadows of the clouds that pass over the earth. He saw the Father's face reflected in the quiet pools . . . and He often closed His eyes to gaze into the Holy Eyes.*
>
> *"The night spoke to Him with the voice of the Father, and in solitude He heard the angel of the Lord calling to Him. And when He stilled Himself in sleep He heard the whispering of the heavens in His dreams."* [1]

Living the spiritual life is not only recognizing the Divine Presence in ourselves—but in *everyone.* It is considering every person *as* their Divine Identity regardless of the situation. And there must be a daily program of meditation on Truth until we feel that Truth entering and filling our hearts. It is a contemplative life of communing with Spirit to such an extent that we actually become Spirit-in-action.

Remember, it is our *awareness-of-Consciousness* that opens the door for the work to be done. What we are conscious of is forever in expression, eternally out-picturing our convictions about ourselves, God, and life. And when our conscious awareness is in the spiritual vibration, as opposed to the disharmony of ego, that which is manifest in the visible world is the Reality of Spirit and not the projection of illusion.

Think on these thoughts:

> *I make the commitment this day to strengthen my awareness, understanding, and knowledge of God, my only Self. I shall do this by loving Spirit with all my mind, heart, and soul. I do this now with the fullness of*

my being.

I acknowledge the Presence within me as the only power at work in my life and affairs. There is no other. Omnipotence, from within out, reigns supreme in my life.

The more I am conscious of Spirit, the more that Spirit fills my consciousness. I focus my mind on the Truth I AM and open the door, and all sense of separation dissolves as I realize my oneness with my Divine Reality. The one Light of love, peace, and understanding anchors Itself in my heart, and I feel the Divine Flame of my Holy Self illuminating my entire being.

From this moment forward, I dedicate my life to Truth. My commitment is complete and is sustained by the will of God.

L E S S O N 6

Rise above Karma

✛   ✛   ✛

Karma is a law of the sleep-state condition arising from the awareness of separate bodies and the perception of relationships. It operates on the dimension of materiality as cause and effect, and serves to maintain the law and order in the illusory world.

Know that in this world, consequence is the law. In spiritual consciousness, there is only Mind and manifestation as one in Spirit without the perception of reward and punishment. In spiritual consciousness, Spirit as Cause expresses Itself as effect in harmonious action without a concept of justice.

Live in spiritual consciousness, and fear not repercussions.

✛   ✛   ✛

The Bible has a great deal to say about karma, or cause and effect, action and reaction. "Judge not, and you will not be judged; condemn not, and you will not be condemned; forgive, and you will be forgiven; give and it shall be given to you; good measure, pressed down, shaken together, running over, will be put into your lap. For the measure you give will be the measure you get back." (Lk 6:37-38) There are many more verses, but this one sums it up best. We always reap what we sow.

I have written in my books—particularly in *The Angels Within Us*—about how to work *with* this law rather than *against* it. "All it takes is discipline and dedication to learn the ancient art of discernment. To be discerning means to be perceptive, astute, discriminating, and judicious. It means to be constantly aware of your thoughts, words, and deeds; and to think, speak, and act only from the standpoint of *harmlessness*."[1]

Good advice, but how many of us can actually put this concept into practice on a day-to-day basis? With great self-control and maximized discipline, we can tip-toe through the mine fields of our self-projected world—always striving to do the right thing—and we might also enjoy life's roller coaster ride, emitting more "Ahs" than screams. But now we understand that we don't have to subject ourselves to that thrill-fright experience. We can rise above the whole business.

The key to this lesson seems to be in where we are sowing, which takes us back to that passage in Galatians 6:8: "For he who sows to his own flesh will from the flesh reap corruption; but he who sows to the Spirit will from the flesh reap eternal life." In other words, if we are casting our seeds—our thoughts and words—into the material world, putting our faith only in the world of effects, the result is going to be a mixed bag of pleasure-pain. But when we sow to Spirit ("sow" meaning "to plant"), depending only on the activity of God in our lives, our mind of awareness is moving into *spiritual consciousness* where only harmony prevails.

In a predominantly material consciousness, we are projecting need thoughts into the world, and need always attracts more need. Fear manifests as fear; harmful actions produce guilt and a call for punishment as karmic payback; a shortcut manipulation to achieve a goal always brings repercussions. When we place our faith only on the world of effects, we are seeking the experience of duality, which, as we will see later, is not real in Divine Consciousness. Yes, we can cast good bread upon the waters, and all that we give is returned, but as long as our intention is to be good simply to reap the benefits of karmic law—without changing our belief system—we're already in trouble. That's tightrope walking with the ego in control, and sometimes that mischievous self-created thought-form forgets about the safety net.

We rise above karmic law when we turn within to the love of God flowing into our conscious awareness as the fulfillment of every need, as the total activity of life. And we become so conscious of Spirit, our only Self, that our awareness of the one Presence and Power overshadows anything on the material plane. That's when the activity of God kicks in as spiritual consciousness, and cause and effect becomes Mind and manifestation—without repayment from either side of the coin. In fact, the coin, as duality, disappears.

> *"In spiritual consciousness there is only Mind and manifestation as one in Spirit without the perception of reward and punishment. In spiritual consciousness, Spirit as Cause expresses Itself as effect in harmonious action without a concept of justice."*

There is only Mind-in-manifestation, a direct-line expression of substance into form and experience, which is always perfect. It is not an "idea" of Spirit that becomes visible; it is Spirit appearing *as* the form—Mind and manifestation as one. And the "illusion" in this sense relates only to the temporary nature of the form as material-physical, and not to ego projections.

A Meditation

I have moved from karmic law to spiritual law, and Spirit is now making my decisions for me from the highest vision.

I feel dramatically different. There is a gentleness combined with an inner strength, a greater sense of peace born of love, and my life is of a higher order.

I am now a healing and harmonizing influence for everyone I encounter on my path through life.

LESSON 7

Understand the Solutions to Problems

You cannot find the solution to a problem in the human mind, for there is not one, the problem or the mind. Yet that which appears to be threatening, when understood as non-power, will disappear into the nothingness from which it came.

Think of a problem or challenge that you may be experiencing at this time. Where did it originate? Out of a belief in two powers—a belief that the Spirit of God within has competition in the outer world of form, an adversary as powerful as Omnipotence itself.

We grew up with this belief. As children, we had battles to fight, pains to alleviate, losses to compensate for, and conditions to overcome. And as we matured into adulthood, these beliefs became even stronger. Oh, we prayed that we would be delivered from the "snare of the fowler and from the noisome pestilence"—

but for the most part, we had to face the challenge and work our way through it to the best of our ability.

Now we hear that not only was there not a problem, but also that there was no human mind to solve it. We created the problem out of our system of false beliefs, and thus it appeared real to us, but there was no substance, energy, or reality behind it. It was nothing but a shadow of beliefs calling for our attention, which we gave it, and made it a part of our reality.

The great metaphysician Emmet Fox once wrote:

> A bogey that you do not believe in has no power to hurt you or worry you. The Bogey Man who lives under the cellar stairs cannot frighten or deceive you *now*, because you do not believe in him; but when you were three years old it was very different. Then he had the power to raise your heartbeat to a gallop. . . . Yet today he cannot cause one flicker of an eyelash—because you do not believe in him. That is the whole difference. Nothing in reality has changed. There is no Bogey Man there, and there never was one at any time; the difference is in you.
>
> Now it is exactly the same with any other kind of evil that may seem to be showing itself in your experience, for all evil is a bogey. It is there only because you believe in it, and it will disappear directly as you cease to believe in it. The only "life" it has is what it receives from you. The only power it has over you is what you give it in belief.[1]

How do we cease believing in bogeys? First, by understanding that in our Divine Consciousness, as exemplified by the Whole Person of the Jesus Model, there never has been or ever will be any sort of difficulty. Second, by becoming consciously aware of the only Self within and letting It change the appearance, which can take place in two ways. In one instance, Spirit "pops the bubble" of the false belief—changes the misqualified energy we are holding—which then reveals to us that there wasn't really a problem in the first place.

For example, when we couldn't get any water out of the faucet, I called the plumber. He checked the water storage tank (we have our own well) and found it empty. He said, "You've got a real problem. Your well has gone dry and you'll have to dig a new one—it will probably cost you about ten grand."

Not good news, but after a deep sigh, I heard the words from within: "Don't fret over a problem that doesn't exist." We called the well company, and after a brief inspection, they found a minor defect in the pump and fixed it for less than a hundred dollars.

Spirit also changes the appearance of the situation by providing what is needed through a change in consciousness. I remember the day a letter from the IRS arrived in the mail demanding much more money than we had available at the time—and they wanted it *immediately*. Now that Bogey Man was very real to me, and I could see him seizing everything we had to pay off the debt. Fear? You bet. So I focused my mind on the Presence within as the solution to the problem. In a few minutes, I heard the inner voice say, "*I am the IRS.*"

What this meant to me was that there was nothing to fear, that every agent was the Spirit of God (omnipresence), and that the belief in a hostile attack from "out there" was being dissolved. I went back in the house and told Jan that everything was okay. No, the IRS didn't forgive the obligation, but three days later, an all-sufficiency of funds came forth to meet it with ease without having to borrow any money. "*. . . that which appears to be threatening, when understood as non-power, will disappear into the nothingness from which it came.*"

A Meditation

This problem that seems to be calling for my attention is something that has been expressed through my belief in two powers. But since Spirit, the only Power, is everywhere present, that means that my life and world are filled with harmony, loving relationships, physical wholeness, true-place success, and lavish abundance.

So where is the problem? It can't be, for it was only a belief, and this error thought is dissolved by Spirit as It flows through me to reveal the Reality of heaven on earth.

I am aware of the activity of Spirit, the only power at work in my consciousness. I feel the shining love, the radiating power, the flow of wisdom. I am as Jesus, and all is well.

L E S S O N   8

Understand True Prayer

*Your Holiness, the Christ, knows all and is
eternally expressing as perfection in individual lives.
Come into alignment with this expression, which is
true prayer. Do not dictate. Consent to the knowingness and activity of Spirit, and be at peace.*

The message here is *omniscience*—the truth that the only Self
knows all, and that the activity of the Self is in constant and
continuous fulfillment without being asked. This gets back to the
natural process of the universe where everything is being maintained at the Divine Standard at all times—wholeness, abundance, right relations, and true success. And that includes each
individual being. Spirit knows our needs, and it is with great love
and joy that every need is met, even before we feel the emotional pressing from the world without.

When we are consciously aware of this truth, we come into alignment with Spirit, and our mind and feeling nature register the sense of *have*. This fulfillment then radiates in, through, and as our consciousness without us having to ask or pray in the traditional way. In fact, petitioning prayer can be a block to the natural order because we are focusing on the problem rather than the solution. We believe that God doesn't know our situation, and we have to inform the Presence of our needs. Also, we are asking for something to be healed in the outer world when the healing only has to take place within, in consciousness.

In my book *With Wings As Eagles,* I wrote:

> The Knowingness of God is the answer to the problem and the fulfillment of the need. Spirit cannot know something without taking action! What Spirit is knowing, It is being, and since Spirit is Omniscient, It is eternally expressing (being) total fulfillment in every area of your life. Do you have a financial, health, relationship or job problem? You can be assured that Spirit knows about it, and that, my friend, is the answer to your prayer.[1]

Yes, Spirit knows, and the activity of Spirit appears in our lives when we are *consciously one* with that Knowingness. We must think as Spirit *knows*—that we are rich, whole, loved, and wonderfully successful. And with those thoughts of I AM and I HAVE—in agreement with our Divine Consciousness—we become the Law of Harmony unto our world. Conversely, when we pray from the ego's fearful perception of lack, sickness, friction, and failure, we are affirming that we *have not*—and "he that hath not, from him shall be taken even that which he hath." That's also the Law in operation, always working in accordance with our beliefs.

Beginning this day, let your prayers be a communion with your glorious Self and an affirmation of the Truth of your Being.

Feel the radiation taking place in and through you—Spirit in expression—and affirm that God loves you, withholds nothing, and is at every moment fulfilling Itself as you, providing everything you could possibly desire. Align your thoughts with Spirit, trust fully, and watch your world turn rightside up again.

A Meditation

I am consciously one with the Infinite Mind within, and through this awareness pulsating throughout my being, I understand Omniscience. My Spirit knows all, sees my every need, and with endless love has already fulfilled that need.

In truth there is nothing to ask for. I simply have to keep my awareness on Omniscience and Its divine activity. This activity is Omnipotent, the one power, pouring forth from me as a mighty fountain to reveal and express a full, complete, and joyous life. I am aware of this. I understand it. I see it. I know it.

See the Highest Vision

You have a choice as to what reality you will experience, for there is more than one door in consciousness. Whichever you choose, your Self will meet you there, either to assist or applaud. Let your choice be the one of your highest ideals, and the vision will be honored.

We know that when we fully realize the Divine Presence, our only Self, our world will be a perfect expression or out-picturing of the Self's will and purpose for a life more abundant. Until then, we will experience various degrees of realization, and with each new understanding, we should have a corresponding demonstration of our Truth of Being. But we still may not be living in complete happiness and harmony. While the sharp turns and falls of the roller coaster have lessened, the ride will seem to continue.

Then what is our responsibility until that moment when we *know that I know*? It is through the continuous practice of *Ideals*—the ideal life in all of its component parts. It is seeing from the highest vision that lifts us up to a higher frequency through which Spirit radiates as our consciousness to manifest equivalent conditions and experiences in life.

I am reminded of the 60-day Non-Human Program as outlined in my book *A Spiritual Philosophy for the New World*. The program will produce miracles as we surrender totally to Spirit in an I-of-myself-can-do-nothing mode and continue with consciousness expansion. But those of you who have gone through the 60-day process know that surrendering is not the end, only the beginning. The whole idea is to break the ego connection and the sense of separation with the only Self, and move into that new altitude of consciousness where you can do all things through a consciousness of the Ideal, and finally to the realization experience where you declare, "I *AM* all things; I am *that* I AM."

Surrendering to the Higher Power and keeping our mind focused on Spirit—on the infinite Knowingness and Activity of our only Self—provides a channel of awareness through which Spirit expresses. However, on what frequency of consciousness are we maintaining that awareness? I can be in a lower frequency—that being my reality at the time—and still be "intellectually" aware of the Presence within, and my Self will assist me in whatever way is appropriate for that level.

The power of God meets us on whatever level of consciousness we may be experiencing at the time. Perhaps another way of saying the same thing is that our world is always a reflection of how we think and feel. That's the way the Law works. The power will work with you, and for you, only as it works *as* you.

For example, a friend of mine was fired from his job and for several days meditated on the Presence within as the way to find the perfect career opportunity—and Spirit met him on the level he was holding in consciousness. He was able to find a job that paid the essential bills, but it was far beneath his talents and abilities. In essence, on some level of consciousness, he chose a reality based on his perception of himself as undeserving and of little value to others. But even on this level of unworthiness, his basic needs were met.

A woman worked with her awareness of Spirit as the channel to bring the right man into her life—and attracted one who gave her many gifts and a new lifestyle of glamour and excitement, but there wasn't any true love in the relationship and it didn't last. The Law of Attraction worked perfectly to correspond to her tone and pitch of consciousness.

The Divine *I* says, "I stand at the door and knock." Being omnipresent in consciousness, our Holiness is at every door—at every possible reality-field in our frequency world. Which door will you open? *"Let your choice be the one of your highest ideals, and the vision will be honored."*

What is your ideal life? What you see, you shall become. I had an experience that showed me that many different realities are always hovering in our energy fields. I was sitting in our living room talking to Jan about a movie we were going to watch later in the evening when suddenly I saw several "discs of energy" floating all around me, each with a luminous tail. The hair on my arms stood straight up, and I silently asked what they were. The answer from within: "These are fields of reality . . . you are in one now . . . some are lower, others higher."

I immediately thought about my life and its various aspects— my physical body, the career I was pursuing, my finances, home, friends, and the degree of fulfillment I felt. And I realized that I was seeing what I considered my "present reality." Was it perfect? Not in every detail. And then I heard, "What is your ideal reality?" As it began to take shape in my mind, the voice said,

"Choose it, live it in consciousness."

Since that time I've understood that every choice we make in life starts a chain reaction that weaves an alternative reality, and that when we change our minds and move in another direction, the previous reality remains. So at all times we have many different "worlds of life" attached to our field of consciousness.

"You have a choice as to what reality you will experience." Those worlds of life might represent a debt-reality, a seemingly factual experience of illness, and what may be considered the truth of failure, broken relationships, loneliness, and sorrow. There's also the life of "getting by"—of managing the good with the bad, of hoping and coping. And most people have experienced the "big-bounce" existence with its feast and famine, ups and down in health, ins and outs of success, wonderful love, and an aftermath of bitter ashes. That's like moving from one reality to another and back again.

What is *your* ideal reality? First, become aware as deeply as you can of Omniscience, understanding that the *I* within knows all and is always the eternal fulfillment. Now move to the truth of Omnipotence—that there is but one power, the power within, and that anything in the outer world is non-power. Then consider Omnipresence, and understand that the infinite Knowingness and Power-for-good is everywhere present in your life.

Now let your consciousness shift to the truth that whatever you can see in mind and feel in heart is already a part of your highest reality. This is the recognition of Have-at-the-present-moment. Now become one with that new reality, giving Spirit the perfect pattern for expression. Capture the image of the perfect body—radiant energy, vibrant, vital, and whole. Don't try to change or improve the body of the other reality by seeing it differently. Rather, accept that Spirit is the only Body, and in your new reality you have only perfection. *I have the Ideal Body.* And what you see on the inner, you shall become in the outer.

See the perfect financial freedom, living completely debt-free and enjoying the fullness of abundance. Don't focus on effects; keep your creative imaging on the screen of your mind, remembering that this is an energy world and that you are working with electromagnetic forces in consciousness. Instead of counting money or seeing yourself spending to your heart's delight, be *one* with the energy of lavish, omnipresent abundance, focusing on the point of contact within that represents perfect finances. *I live in Ideal Wealth!*

See your highest ideal of creative success. Focus only on perfection in relationships. Feel the perfect environment of the ideal home. Reach for the highest vision of life in all its aspects, hold the vision, and let it be absorbed in consciousness as the pattern of perfection.

I mentioned the ideal home above, which brings up an interesting story. Just before we moved ourselves and the Quartus staff from Austin to Boerne, Jan and I were devoting time daily to the 60-day Non-Human Program, which means that we had surrendered the entire moving experience to Spirit. Everything went as smooth as silk, except early on we couldn't find the right house for us. So Jan went into meditation and heard the words, "I go before you to prepare a place for you." What kind of a place? Jan didn't specify a particular form of architecture, style, arrangement of rooms, or the look of the surroundings. From the assurance, she simply knew that we already had the Ideal Home, and in her imaging faculty she saw us joyfully living and playing with our dog Maggi in the perfect dwelling—and she let the Ideal be absorbed in consciousness.

Before we drove back to Boerne to look again, Jan called the Realtor there and asked about a certain area outside of town. We wanted to *lease* a house, and the Realtor told her there were only homes for *sale* there, and then described a particular home.

Jan said, "We want to look at it." The Realtor agreed, but said the owner would let the house rot before he would lease it. We went to see it anyway, and when we walked in, we knew it was our home. It had a private study for me, a room for Jan to work when not at the office, two living areas, and it was situated on three beautiful tree-filled acres with a swimming pool. I told the Realtor to make a lease-offer on the house and specified what we were prepared to pay. She did, and was shocked when the owner accepted. A couple of years later, we bought the home for $75,000 under the appraised price. *Ideals* in consciousness work miracles!

On January 1, 1997, Jan wrote in her journal:

"Moving into inner space, I contemplate the ending year. What do I wish to let go, to leave behind in 1996 as I tred the fresh snow of '97? I see that what must be let go of is 'the belief in' whatever I choose to leave behind, for the 'belief in' is what causes 'the manifestation of.' So I let go of the belief that there is or can be any kind of limitation. I let go of the belief that anyone is wrong, that anyone is without love and fulfillment. I let go of the belief in stress, tension, discord, illness, aging; that there is any lack of time or energy. I let go of the belief that I do not live in a perfect, harmonious, joyous, prosperous, loving world. I LIVE IN A PERFECT WORLD. Not much more needs to be said."

Let go of false "beliefs in" and find your perfect world, and know that everything seen and felt in mind and heart is real. It's yours now in deep awareness, and don't let anything sway you from the vision. It is your present reality, a force field for perfection in every detail. Live it. Be it. And Spirit will do the rest.

A Meditation

I move into a New Reality now, my Ideal Life where everything is perfect. I turn within and see and know and feel the Ideal Body of pure energy—whole, radiant, and filled with the one Life of Spirit. I live the Body-Ideal.

I live and move and have my being in lavish abundance, and I see only from the highest vision the wholeness and completeness of my financial affairs. I live the Abundance-Ideal.

I see my Ideal of perfect creative success, and in the spirit of Have, I know that what I see I shall become. I am the fullness of perfect achievement, of total victory and triumph. I live the Success-Ideal.

My relationships are perfect, for I am loving and loved, and I see myself as everyone. I give to all the happiness and harmony that I AM and HAVE, which is overflowing and unending. I live the Relationship-Ideal.

Every other detail in my life is perfect. This is now my Reality, and I watch as my world reflects this perfection. I live the Life-Ideal.

Know the One
Healing Presence

✛   ✛   ✛

Only the Spirit of God can heal, That which you are,
for It is the activity of the one Life which is perfect.
Nothing is impossible when you know the meaning
of omnipresent Life and the non-power of effects.
Understand and be aware of the radiating energy
of the Word of God as the Law of Wholeness.
Be the healing power.

✛   ✛   ✛

Because of the seeming worldwide need for physical healings on a daily basis, I will offer additional research and an in-depth interpretation for this particular lesson. Healing is a part of the natural order process, and we are all healers. Therefore, we must understand—without a shadow of a doubt—that *nothing is impossible.* The restoration of our minds, emotions, and bodies to the Divine Standard is an activity of our Holy Self working *through* our awareness of Its Presence and Power. And regardless of the condition that our false beliefs have created, it can be corrected. "There is no order of difficulty." The same principle holds true for healing others. When we are aware of our Divine Identity—and any other particular person as the *I-Spirit-Life* of God—the *I* of that individual is released from false beliefs to do its healing work. This is the true significance of *omnipresence*.

When Jan had her massive heart attack and was pronounced clinically dead, she traveled beyond the veil, experienced the fullness of her Self, and was able to return with a heightened awareness and understanding of her true nature. And her return to this plane and her speedy recovery was due in part to many people moving up into that realm of *I-Spirit-Life*, thus accelerating the primary intention in her physical system. Since then, she has had the opportunity to demonstrate the one healing presence and power that is within us all.

At different times and locations, men and women complaining of severe headaches were touched by her, and the pain immediately went away. A friend of ours went to the doctor and was told she had a large tumor. When she went back a few weeks later, it was gone. What had happened? Her mother had called Jan, who immediately went into meditation, knowing that there is only one Universal Self—the true and perfect Self of everyone. In her deep awareness of the single *I*, she saw the malady as a non-power with no law to sustain it; therefore, it could not be real. But Jan knew she wasn't the healing power; she was simply a point in omnipresence. In Spirit, she and the woman were one, and Jan's understanding of that truth released the healing power to reveal the reality of wholeness.

Throughout the ages, there have been demonstrations of incredible healings—not by a personal mind, but by the omnipresent *I* working *through* the healers. To all outward appearances, these healers are considered normal human beings, yet they have realized their inner power and are able to perform seeming miracles. Jan and I have witnessed such miracles first-hand, and a large number of case histories have been recorded by the American Academy of Parapsychology and Medicine, the American Medical Association, the National Institute of Physiology in Moscow, the British Medical Association, and the Vatican's Medical Commission.

They include a woman seeing through "dead eyes" after the severing of the optic nerve, the instantaneous removal of cancerous growths, mysterious cures of essentially every form of disease, the healing of all manner of wounds—some considered "mortal"—without medical assistance, the fleshing out of a withered leg in seconds, and the return to normalcy of those considered mentally retarded. *"Nothing is impossible when you understand the meaning of omnipresence and the non-power of effects."*

I can remember as a little boy being shocked at cowboys being killed by bullets in a movie. *That can't happen,* I thought—the body should be able to heal itself. I watched that movie four times, hiding under the seat between showings, trying to figure out what was wrong. (My mother thought I had been kidnaped and called the sheriff.) Perhaps I had tapped in to some ancient memory that reminded me that Life is constantly creating a body, and you can't kill Life.

Later, during the 1940s, I heard many "war stories"—some bordering on the mystical and mysterious, others outright incredible, such as the spontaneous healing of bullet and shrapnel wounds by "some unknown force." You might also want to talk to doctors and nurses in a hospital emergency room and ask if anything phenomenal or paranormal ever occurs. If you can find one who will confide in you, chances are that he or she will speak in confidence of "puzzling" situations where a person experienced a sudden and unexplained healing.

Author Joseph J. Weed tells about the healing of a dog by "an advanced student" in his book *Wisdom of the Mystic Masters*:

One day as I was walking in the country with my dog, an Irish setter, he flushed a rabbit and chased it into the brush. In his excitement he ran into a dead bush and one of the branches broke off in his eye. It was horrible to look at, with the end of the broken branch sticking out of his eye and a few drops of blood running from it. Calling him to me, I took his head in my lap and with a quick jerk removed the sharp branch. The wound was large and gaping but I held him quiet and gave him several positive treatments, directing the energy into the spine directly back of the head and at the same time visualizing it flowing into the eye and healing it.

After about ten minutes, I lifted his head and looked at the eye. The bleeding had stopped and the wound was much smaller. I could see then quite plainly that the hole was in the lower portion of the eyeball beneath the pupil. With him on leash to keep him quiet, we started for home, nearly an hour's walk. He appeared in no distress and trotted quietly beside me. When we reached the house, another look showed the wound down to almost a pinpoint, and the following morning there was no trace, not even a scar.[1]

A man we knew suffered a serious leg injury that had solidified as a result of many bone grafts, and it was the size of a broomstick. In an experience "in the Light," the leg was fleshed out and made perfect again—an instantaneous healing with complete regeneration of bone and tissue. And this case was fully documented by his wife and friends.

In Michael Talbot's book *The Holographic Universe,* he documents the case history of Vittorio Michelli and the regeneration of bone—an impossibility, according to the medical community. However, as the Vatican's Medical Commission stated in its official report: "A remarkable reconstruction of the iliac bone cavity has taken place. The X rays made in 1964, 1965, 1968 and 1969 confirm categorically and without doubt that an unforeseen and even overwhelming bone reconstruction has taken place of a type unknown in the annals of world medicine."[2]

Talbot also tells about Marin Dajo, a fencing foil stuck "completely through his body, clearly piercing vital organs but causing Dajo no harm or pain. . . . when the foil was removed, Dajo did not bleed and only a faint red line marked the spot where the foil had entered and exited."[3] In this case, Dajo had complete control of his own body, but it shows once again that *nothing is impossible.*

There is also the remarkable healing of Sigrun Seutemann. She was involved in a "head-on collision with a large truck [that] crushed the front half of her car to the extent that it was necessary to cut it apart in order to get her out of the wreckage. She was horribly mangled with what later were found to be 18 fractures. Her ankle was crushed. Her forehead from the eyebrows up into the hair was sliced into ribbons, and the entire skin which had been below the jaw, was now a flap folded down onto her chest. She was adjudged to be dying from loss of blood."[4] While Seutemann's healing cannot be called instantaneous, her recovery was miraculous, thanks to the healers who worked with her. She improved so dramatically that plastic surgery was not needed and she was soon walking without a limp.

Miraculous healings have taken place throughout ancient times, and the four gospels are filled with individual and multiple healings by Jesus. Let's begin with the dead child in Luke 8:53-55: "And they laughed at him, knowing that she was dead. But taking her by the hand he called, saying, 'Child, arise.' And her spirit returned, and she got up at once, and he directed that something should be given her to eat." Now remember Jesus' statement in John 14:12 about us doing "even greater works than these."

In the *Decline and Fall of the Roman Empire*, author Edward Gibbon reported that during the first century of Christianity, the lame walked, the blind saw, the sick were healed, and the dead were raised, the latter considered a common event. And there's the story of Saint Francis of Assisi (1182–1226) healing a leper:

> Said St. Francis, "That which thou desirest I will do." . . . thereafter he undressed him and began to wash him with his own hands, while another friar poured on the water; and by Divine Miracle, where St. Francis touched him with his holy hands, the leprosy departed and the flesh remained perfectly sound.[5]

And the miracles continued, but it was not until the early part of this century that research began on what might be called "paranormal" healings. In the book *Healers and the Healing Process* (edited by George W. Meek), a report on ten years of research by 14 world-famous investigators, we read:

> Almost two-thirds of the adult body is composed of water. . . . The significance of this for our understanding of healing is that water is extremely sensitive to many types of radiations. The American industrial research scientist Robert N. Miller and physicist Prof. Phillip B. Reinhart have now devised four separate instrumental means to show that some of the energy flowing from a healer's hands can trigger an alteration of the molecular bond between the hydrogen and oxygen molecules in water."[6]

There is also a report from the Delawarr Laboratories in England where tap water was photographed by a radionic camera, and a normal molecular structure was shown. However, when the water was *blessed*, there was a completely different energy pattern. If we think of water as a particular liquid energy that constitutes most of our composition, and that this energy is highly susceptible to the healing/blessing power, we can see how a touch or radiation from hands can produce a dramatic effect—particularly when the healer is attuned to his or her Divine Consciousness. I feel this was the case when Jan touched the people with the severe headaches. Eighty percent of the head area is nothing but "extremely sensitive" water!

"Understand and be aware of the radiating energy of the Word of God as the Law of Wholeness. Be the healing power." To understand what happens, let's look at the quote by Professor William Tiller of Stanford University in *Healers and the Healing Process*:

> Through mind forces, one can create a pattern, and that pattern then acts as a force field which applies to the next level of substance. In turn, that force field is a force for organizing the atoms and molecules into configurations at that level of substance. That pattern of substance at the etheric level, then, is a particular state of organization and it has its own radiation field—its own force field if you like—and that force field then, is a field for the organization of matter at the next level of substance—the physical level of substance. These etheric forces, then, bring about the coalescence and organization of matter at the physical level of substance.[7]

This relates specifically to information I received while meditating one day on what I called the Healing Principle. The inner voice said, *"Bodies are five, but five is not. The first is the eternal spiritual nature of perfection. Heal the confusion of the second, the mental body, and the mind is clear. Heal the plane of the third, the emotional body, and the emotions are stilled. Heal the sheath of the fourth, the etheric body, and the physical is well."*

The initial healing pattern, created by a deep awareness of the Holy *I* within—with or without a touch of hands—takes place in the mental body, that realm of energy in closest proximity to Divine Consciousness. There it produces a force field that "applies to the next level of substance." This continues until it reaches the etheric body, which then organizes the atoms and molecules for the physical level.

Again, what is the motivating force, the primary intention, for all of this? The only Self we have, the Master *I*—omniscient, omnipotent, and omnipresent. As I've said, we are all healers, and the greater the realization of Who and What we are, the greater the healing power, for ourselves and others.

Jan once wrote to members of the Quartus Society, the membership organization of the Quartus Foundation: "Let's heal the sick. We have the power and I'm not afraid to try. Maybe at first we won't do it in great significant ways, but it is time to begin. . . . Each time we try and accomplish in a small way, it opens the door for a greater demonstration."

I feel this is particularly true when we apply the principles contained in the Jesus Code.

A Meditation

I am a healing power for others, for I am omnipresent, one with all in the unity of all life. I see everyone as my Self, and the power is released to reveal the reality of wholeness.

I let the Light of Spirit go before me now to prove that nothing is impossible, as It establishes the force field for wholeness regardless of the situation or condition. The Divine Intention of Spirit never fails.

I am a healing influence wherever I go, and whomever I touch feels the mighty radiation of Spirit. I am You and You are Me, and we are one eternally in the Wholeness of Perfection.

LESSON 11

Heal Thyself

✠   ✠   ✠

The body is maintained in wholeness when you live in and as higher Consciousness. Open to the Healing Presence, the One Power, and be whole. Limit not your vision to see perfection. Unite with the purpose of Love, and receive the inflow. Feel the energy as purifying Light throughout the entire body.

Disease is true only to your belief. Shall you be healed of that which is real and yet is not? Know that only thoughts and emotions require healing. Consent to healing. Acquiesce. Let the effect of the emotional thought-wound be healed by Love.

✠   ✠   ✠

Again, we see how essential it is to live in and as the *I* of our being and see only the Body-Ideal. In essence, what we think of as a physical body is a sculptured pillar of light—pure, pulsating energy incorporating the perfect pattern for the manifestation of what we perceive to be as form. But the reality of our world is pure energy, and as we move into higher consciousness, we will see the ethereal appearance of solid structure, as the energy pattern behind the form begins to show through. This "shining reality" also reveals to us that there is no decay, disease, or aging within the energy configuration, and as we hold that perception in our minds, the object seen as solid begins to reflect its true perfection. This process can be simulated through abstract thinking—in other words, seeing a physical body as a pure field of light through the imaging faculty of mind (imagination).

Remember that we have created our objective world through focused consciousness. At the point where light and lens of mind meet, we took clear and sharply defined pictures of objective life as we perceived our personal world to be. And what developed were energy patterns that we "froze" in time and space to appear as form and experience. Many times, however, our focus was inverse creation, and we took pictures we did not want to develop. For example, when an affliction appeared in the body, we energized it even more and carried it into full disease by focusing on the problem, seeing it worsening. And so it did. The key here is to focus only on the perfection of our Being. Let's go back to the "beginning" now and see how the physical form was created.

In the dim recesses of the ancient past, an archetype of the body was imaged in consciousness—an original pattern or model of atomic structure in an energy field, which became visible to us through mind action. The prototype included all that was necessary to live in the elements of the denser physical plane, and from this pattern, light waves radiated as lines of force causing an atomic cluster. This resulted in cells forming tissues, organs, a life stream we call blood, a muscular organ to pump it, an organ of external respiration to give the blood its oxygen supply, an organ to cleanse the blood, a digestive system, a skeletal-muscular system, and so forth—all becoming visible on an extremely narrow range on the electromagnetic spectrum. Yet the entire body is nothing more than energy in motion, "whispy fluff." And as we discussed earlier, we originally had the ability to change the molecular structure and eliminate the appearance of the form.

Again, we are not a body, but we *have* one while on this plane of existence. And the body can be maintained in the degree of perfection corresponding to our awareness, understanding, and knowledge of the *I-Spirit-Self*. It is the omniscience and omnipotence of *I* that takes care of everything—when we are aligned with that Divine Consciousness in thoughts and feelings—until it is our time to "lay it down" and return to our natural abode.

Our objective is to continually release the body to perfect Life, see it as an activity of Life, and let it be governed accordingly. The body is pure energy, but when we see it as something else, focus on the malady, and try to heal an organ through thought, we are accepting the idea that there is a physical problem, thus separating ourselves even more from the power of Divine Consciousness. The body cannot be sick, because "sickness" does not exist at any point in the universe. It only appears to come forth through a false belief, which is not real. Therefore, less-than-perfect health exists only as a thought-form, and not as a reality.

False Beliefs Cause the Appearance of Illness

The primary thorn in consciousness is the belief in two powers, which then splinters out into such beliefs as separation from our Source, a punishing God who wills sickness, a malevolent universe, karma, and heredity—which lead to judgment, criticism, anger, unforgiveness, guilt, unrestrained desires, and self-pity.

In the one Mind, Omnipresent *I*, which includes all there is anywhere and everywhere, there is only the single Omnipotence— an infinite Will-for-Good. There is no other power. And it is impossible for us to be separated from our Source, because we are that

Source in conscious Self-awareness. There is no other God, which means we live in a totally benevolent universe.

English psychologist Charles F. Haanel has written:

> There are those who seem to think that sickness and suffering are sent by God; if so, every physician, every surgeon and every Red Cross nurse is defying the will of God, and hospitals are places of rebellion instead of houses of mercy. . . . Theology has been trying to teach an impossible Creator, one who created beings capable of sinning and then allowed them to be eternally punished for such sins. Of course, the necessary outcome of such extraordinary ignorance was to create fear instead of love. . . . [1]

And Karma? We have seen that it is nothing more than cause and effect on the lower plane, which we rise above when we accept our divinity—as simple as stepping out of the gutter and up onto the curb. And heredity? When we incarnate, we do attach ourselves to a particular genealogical energy field, but with God as the fathering element of life, how can we inherit anything but perfection?

We must change our minds and see only Truth, which means the ability to see the non-power of appearances. When we stop fearing what's going on in the body, we stop judging, which opens the way for the Omnipotent *I* to reveal the reality behind the illusion.

Let's pause for a moment for a meditation.

What is this in my body calling for attention? It is a false belief that has been projected into my physical vehicle. I know that my body does not have the power to be sick, for it has no mind of its own. It is simply partaking of misqualified energy, which is giving the appearance of a malady.

I now turn within to my only Self, the I that I AM, and rest in the assurance that Omniscience and Omnipotence are maintaining my body in perfect wholeness. I connect my gaze to the all-knowing Presence, the one Power, and let the shining Light of Love move through my mental and emotional systems, dissolving false beliefs and healing the error patterns that I have created.

I now see only the Ideal Body, a pure energy field of perfection, absolute wholeness, radiant light—totally governed, maintained, and sustained by the Spirit of the Living God.

The lesson in this chapter also deals with using creative imaging to dissolve false beliefs. *"Limit not your vision to see perfection."* The concept here is that "energy follows thought"—a basic teaching in the Sacred Academies of the past. But understand that this doesn't mean thought manipulation to change something in the physical system. Rather, it is using our minds to see only the perfection that already exists—that is, *there is nothing to heal.*

Here is a healing exercise based on the lesson that Jan and I frequently use. *"Unite with the purpose of Love, and receive the inflow."* We do this beginning with the energy center above the top of the head (crown), seeing the energy descending as purifying Love-Light throughout the entire body. Do it yourself, seeing and feeling the flow of energy. As this Love-Light flows down, it transmutes the negative energy; it breaks the hold of the false belief. And through your imaging faculty, you are given the picture of a "light body"—that which you truly are. And the more you hold that image, the more the physical form functions on a higher level.

Creative imagination is such a powerful force (the vision to see perfection) that energy can be directed and points of friction in the auric field eliminated, thus relieving the pressure on the physical system. For example, most physical ailments are caused by disturbances in the emotional body, that band of energy surrounding the physical and pressing on the etheric. Do a "radar sweep" of your emotions and pick up the blips—those reactionary feelings of fear, guilt, resentment, suppressed desires, unworthiness, and self-condemnation. Now in your mind's eye, fashion a laser beam of love-light, and send it to that identified bogey and see it eliminated instantly. It will be because *energy follows thought!* And keep beaming the rays until you feel clean and clear again.

Another exercise is to find where the darkened energy is manifesting as sickness in the physical. After discovering this technique, we have used it in our workshops with dramatic results. First, determine the corresponding energy center (chakra) serving as entrance to the affected area. Let's say you're having stomach problems. The corresponding center to the stomach is the solar plexus chakra. With your imaging faculty, see the light moving through that chakra, bathing the stomach with its brilliance. *"Let the effect of the emotional thought-wound be healed by love."* In other words, consent to a healing of the emotional thought-form that has been projected into the stomach, and not the stomach itself.

If the malady is in the head area, bring in the light from the third-eye chakra between the brows. Neck and throat, the throat chakra. Heart and lungs, the heart chakra. Between the navel to the reproductive organs, the sacral chakra. And from the base of the spine on down to the feet, the root chakra.

After about a minute of concentrated focus, withdraw the light, for further attention to the afflicted area is not necessary and could produce agitation. Our experience has shown us that the first treatment is usually enough, and then we get our minds off the discomfort and get back firmly in the conscious awareness of the *I-Self*. If it is a chronic situation, two treatments a day is recommended, with additional meditation on releasing the physical system to the Governing *I*.

On another occasion, while contemplating physical fitness, I had a flow-through of thoughts that said in effect, *Let your exercise be to the rhythm of the universe . . . seek not physical stress. Let the fitness of body be revealed through fitness of mind, yet exercise of muscles contributes to poise, presence, and balance of mind. Let body and mind work in unison.*

I felt that this was a direct reference to Tai Chi exercises, which are in tune with the natural order and the "rhythm of the universe." This ancient method of physiological renewal is highly effective in healing and in the retardation of aging. The idea is to work with forces of energy to harmonize breath and cultivate greater energy circulation through the acupuncture meridians.

You may also want to develop your own rhythmic exercises, such as motion with meditation as you let Spirit move your body. Or as Jan tells me each day when she heads down our country lane, "I am going to walk the body." Think about that statement. It puts everything into the proper perspective.

LESSON 12

Understand That
Scarcity Has
No Reality

*Why do you believe in scarcity? Abundance can be
visibly manifest, but scarcity cannot. Lack has no
reality, and the belief that it does must be changed.*

We must understand that scarcity, shortages, lack, and limitation are but shadows of the reality of abundance, and
shadows can never be real. Scarcity cannot be manifest. Nothing
cannot become something. Zero times zero is zero.

The infinite nonphysical universe is literally bursting with the
creative energy of abundance and finds its outlet for expression
by individualizing as each one of us, and then radiates out
through our consciousness into manifest form and experience. So
on the invisible side, we have everything—our world is totally
complete.

When we look at our visible world, we find the same thing. It has been said that if all the manifest money was divided equally among all the people on earth, each one of us would be super-billionaires. (But those without the *consciousness* for wealth would soon lose it to those who did.) And Mother Nature shows us that she certainly doesn't believe in scarcity. Look around you.

But what about the destitute people in the world? And how about those who have been prosperous only to find themselves suddenly in a dark hole of insufficiency? It gets back to that belief in scarcity again—or the possibility that it can, at one time or another, rear its ugly head and take charge of our lives. Those in what appears to be concretized poverty will be released when the collective mind shifts into spiritual reality. And the in-and-out prosperity people can get back on the abundance track by changing personal beliefs. Remember the lesson: *"Lack has no reality, and the belief that it does must be changed."*

If we try to improve our lives by attempting to manipulate effects (rather than change beliefs), we are digging a deeper hole of scarcity for ourselves. In the lower frequencies of consciousness, we can't do a thing except perhaps bring some minor relief to a situation. The only real change in the outer-world situation will be made by spiritual consciousness—a mind that knows there is only one Mind—consciousness in oneness with Spirit-Self, focusing inwardly and releasing outwardly. Remember, we don't have to *get* anything. We only have to *give* by releasing the flow of energy outward. With purpose of mind, we radiate the energy—pour, give, and send forth.

Think on these thoughts:

I am the Spirit of God in individual expression. Therefore, all that God is, I AM. I am the embodiment of all the energies of God, including abundance. I am abundance. I am lavish abundance, and I let it flow forth now. I am the flow of wealth.

> *I am the principle of abundance, the law of supply,*
> *and the activity of the law—the very love of God—is*
> *constantly shining through the identity of abundance I*
> *am holding before it. I am shining abundance.*

Praying for money can limit the outpouring of the energy of abundance into manifest expression. Our prayers should be meditations for a deeper awareness of the Presence within, a greater understanding of the kingdom we've been given—the Ideal Abundance—and a clearer knowledge of how the law works.

The Presence is our reality. It is the only Self there is. Each one of us is infinite Divine Consciousness with total dominion over this world. We are pure Spirit, the Light of God.

The kingdom we've been given is the allness of everything we could possibly desire. Within our consciousness are the ideas corresponding to everything in the physical world. One of these ideas is money, and Spirit *as* our consciousness is continually expressing Itself as visible supply. The process can only be stopped by a belief in scarcity. Where is the scarcity? It cannot be manifest, so there isn't any. It is only a belief.

The law, or principle, is the activity of the one Self. This activity is energy-in-motion; it is shining light, flowing substance, the love of God in action moving from Mind into manifestation through our consciousness. As we believe in our heart, it is done unto us. Feelings of love and faith always override emotions of fear and doubt, and open the channel for the energy flow.

A Word about Faith

When we fear something, we are placing our faith in two powers, which is a lie. We believe that there is something or someone out there who has power over us, and all prayers (what we are holding in consciousness) are answered in accordance to where the faith is placed. If we are focusing our faith on problems, we are intensifying the problems because that is what we're praying for—and in doing so, we are denying the loving will of God and the truth that there is but one Presence and Power in this universe.

To paraphrase Paul, faith is the energy of that which is to be manifest. Therefore, when we focus our faith on our true Identity, on the kingdom that was given to us with great pleasure, and on the law-for-good that is eternally in operation, then we open ourselves to the wonderful experiences of life. Then our prayers are always answered because we believe they are. Here is one based on Truth that we can all believe, and therefore is quickly answered.

> *I am the Spirit of God I AM. I am the Spirit of God I AM as lavish abundance. I am the Spirit of God I AM as lavish abundance in radiant expression in my life and affairs.*
>
> *Money is a spiritual idea in my consciousness. This idea is unlimited; therefore, the expression of the idea in visible form is unlimited. I am the spiritual law governing this spiritual idea. I am the principle of abundance. I am the radiating energy of abundance, and I let this energy fill my world and return unto me as an all-sufficiency of money and every other good thing. I am radiating the energy and love of God. I am attracting that which is mine by right of consciousness.*
>
> *I no longer let my mind and emotions dwell on scarcity, for I know that no such thing exists. I place my faith in God, on the Spirit I AM, on the well of abundance that is ever flowing from the divine fountain within, and on the divine process of perfect manifestation.*
>
> *I dismiss all thoughts of delay, all beliefs that my good shall appear when I am more spiritual, more*

deserving, a better person. The law of supply works in the NOW, in the present moment. The instant I felt the need, the intelligent all-loving creative energy flowing from the center of my being knew exactly what to do to fulfill the need. And through this prayer of faith, that love of God in action is released to do its mighty work.

And it is so.

LESSON 13

Understand the Nature of Supply

✚　✚　✚

Supply is all-inclusive. It is that from which ALL form, ALL things, ALL experiences come forth; nothing is missing. It is the energy of spiritual love. It is Mother-Substance, the Divine Mother, flowing through receptive spiritual awareness that manifests as completeness in life.

✚　✚　✚

Many on the spiritual path know that invisible supply as spiritual consciousness is the source and cause of the visible effect we call money, but now we understand that supply literally appears as everything—food, clothing, houses, cars, jobs, friends, love-mates, health, peace, protection—whatever is required for a life more abundant. Supply is *all-inclusive.*

Equating supply with the Divine Mother-Substance also puts it into a context that helps us understand that we are forever nourished, protected, and cared for by a gentle, loving, devoted, and sheltering aspect of our own divinity, which brings it into a very personal relationship, as opposed to impersonal energy.

Contemplate the presence of the Divine Mother-Substance now. Her gaze is upon you; your conscious awareness is the focus of her love. She is omniscient, which means that she knows every empty pocket in mind, every need that has been registered in heart. She reads you as an open book and knows exactly what to do to bring everything up to the divine standard in your life. Her streams of energy flow in accordance with your conscious receptivity to her creative activity.

Ageless Wisdom describes the Mother as the third aspect of divinity, the Holy Spirit, the intelligence of substance, and the nature of form. It is "the bringing together of spirit and matter upon the physical plane. The third aspect is . . . the creator aspect and the energy which produces the outer tangible plane of manifestation—the form side of life."[1]

I also appreciated the idea that supply is *the energy of love*, which relates to another statement from the Wisdom Teachings: "Remember that money is the consolidation of the loving, living energy of divinity, and the greater the realization and expression of love, the freer will be the inflow of that which is needed to carry forward the work."[2]

I remembered the dream I wrote about in *A Spiritual Philosophy for the New World*, where an old man came to me and said, "If you would only love more, all limitations in your life will vanish."[3] Love truly is the energy and cause behind all manifestation, and love is what Jesus came to teach, as echoed by Paul: "God's love has been poured into our hearts through the Holy Spirit which has been given to us." (Rom. 5:5)

This lesson also reminded me that if we are experiencing financial lack, we are focusing on the scarcity of supply in material form. Supply is spiritual, our conscious awareness of Mother-Substance. To focus primarily on the appearance without the consciousness of supply that expresses as the form is fruitless. Same thing for anything else in the phenomenal world. Most problems in life can be traced to our mental and emotional concentration on the realm of effects rather the kingdom of cause, which is the Mother-Substance.

I was told one day in meditation that another meaning for *kingdom* was "substance." With this in mind, let's substitute the words in a few passages from the Bible.

The *substance* of heaven is at hand. (Mt. 3:2)

But first seek the *substance* of God . . . and all these things shall be added unto you. (Mt. 6:33)

. . . inherit the *substance* prepared for you from the foundation of the world. (Mt. 25:34)

Unto you it is given to know the mysteries of the *substance* of God. (Lk. 8:10)

The *substance* of God is come nigh unto you. (Lk. 10:9)

" . . . behold, the *substance* of God is within you. (Lk. 17:21)

I wrote in *The Superbeings:*

As the substance idea is understood and realized, every need of supply in the physical world is made manifest. Substance—flowing through a consciousness of substance— "reads your needs" as it passes through your mind and literally becomes the needed thing, whether money, a home, an automobile, or whatever.[4]

Think of substance now as the kingdom of God within, the very *love* of God, infinite and omnipresent *supply*, omniscient and omnipotent *energy*, and the *Divine Mother* who expresses in and as consciousness from the invisible to the visible.

The Tibetan Master, Djwhal Khul, comments on the phrase *Mother of the World* as meaning "the feminine aspect of manifestation, symbolized for us in many world religions as a virgin mother and in the Christian religion as the Virgin Mary. It is that substance which enables Deity to manifest."[5]

Meditate on being receptive to the Mothering aspect within. Accept that loving energy, substance, the great love of God in action, and return that love with great adoration. Get a feel, an understanding, of your energy field as all-inclusive supply. See with the mind's eye the currents of pulsating energy; feel the throbbing love; be one with the dynamo of creative power flowing through you.

Now ponder these ideas:

It is God's love embodied in my consciousness that is doing the work. I relax into Mother-Substance and let love do everything for me, as me. It knows exactly what to do and is doing it now.

I do not go to God for material things. I turn within and become receptive to the flow of Mother-Love, and let my love-consciousness manifest as total fulfillment in my life.

Jan and I have found over the years that we cannot depend on yesterday's supply for today. There must be a new receptivity to the inflow each and every day. Do that now. Knowing that energy follows thought, reach within to that inner door, beyond which lies the fullness of Divine Consciousness.

With purpose of mind, open the door and release the forces of Mother-Substance-Love, seeing and feeling that dynamic, omniscient energy fill your consciousness. Then see it going before you to straighten every crooked place and manifest as wholeness and perfection in every area of life.

Now take the following statements into meditation:

I am as Jesus, one with the mothering aspect of my divinity. I open the door to this eternal love, God's love for me, and I feel it pouring into my conscious awareness.

I have been given everything, and I know with all my heart that God's love as Mother-Substance is appearing as every needed thing in my life.

I know this. I accept this, for it is the Truth.

L E S S O N   1 4

Do Not Depend on Anything in the External World

*Effects do not produce effects, for they represent
the past and not the now. No person, place, thing,
condition, or situation in the external world
has power over you or to create anew for you.
Place your undivided dependence on Spirit within,
and Love will meet your needs.*

This lesson appears to be a continuation from the previous one and deals with our conscious awareness of the activity of Spirit within, the Divine I AM Identity of the Jesus Model. When we are not in *spiritual* awareness, we are living in a mindfulness of the external world with all its pain, scarcity, conflict, and sorrow.

In material consciousness, we are dealing with the world of effects, which represents the past. What we see is already manifest, much from the influence of the collective consciousness. In this lower frequency, our dependence shifts to certain people who we feel have power over us, or we assume will be responsible for our good—people such as husbands and wives, bankers, employers, mentors, friends and relatives, representatives of the government—and in my case, I would also include agents, editors, publishers, booksellers, and buyers.

First, no one in the outer world has power over you unless you give it to them, which makes them the ruler and you the victim. To be fearful of others is to give them your energy. To be angry with someone is to become negatively attached to that person. The only power on earth is within you, so begin right now to withdraw your projections of fear, anger, and subservience on others. The Spirit within you is your power and authority. In spiritual consciousness, there is no rank, so see everyone else as the Holy Self they are in truth, and get on equal terms with the universal family. *We are as Jesus.*

In the same vein, think what happens when we look to others for our joy and fulfillment. It's like taking that old roller coaster ride with many ups and downs. We expect much, and in happy anticipation we look for positive answers, rich benefits, love and caring, and right action. Then we become frustrated with others' words, suspicious of their motives, angry with their actions, and depressed over dead-end appearances.

Yes, people can be helpful to us, but it is only when we place our total dependence on Spirit within that those who are attuned in some way to our energy field—to our purpose in life—are divinely influenced in a cooperative spirit of helpfulness. If we try to use "mind power" to act upon someone, to sway them in our favor in a me-win game, we're initiating a form of black magic that will backfire on us.

Even if it's a relatively simple act of trying to *get* something from another person—to use subtle leverage to have him or her fulfill a particular need for us—we are removing ourselves from the loving, omnipresent activity of God. But when we live in an awareness of Spirit within, that mind-energy works through our Self-awareness to touch others and bring forth harmony and divine order for the good of all concerned.

Let's consider other areas of the external world where we have placed our faith, our dependence. I've had people tell me that if only they could move to another city, everything would be great in their lives. But we must remember that we always take our consciousness with us, and if we are unhappy in one location, chances are we'll experience that state of mind in another. Again, the key to life is *spiritual awareness, spiritual understanding, spiritual knowing.* When our entire reliance is placed on Spirit within, any geographic change will be Spirit's responsibility— and we may very well be guided to move, perhaps to some place we had never considered, but the end result will be a delightful experience in the adventure of life.

We have also placed our dependence on money, our job or profession, the right partner to live with, retirement plans and "nest eggs" for the future—on down to the food we eat, the medicines we take, a particular climate, and a safe home-neighborhood environment. In truth, there is nothing in the external world that can give us security, fulfillment, health, and happiness. We can enjoy the effects and the relationships, but only if they emanate from the activity of Love within and not from manipulation, the striving-to-get consciousness of ego-materiality, or the illusions of so-called safe conditions.

When our focus is on Truth, Spirit, Self, Substance, and Love, we're living in the Now, and we become the channels for the will of God, the purpose of Self, and the manifestation of Spirit. We totally trust the inner dynamic process and behold Love in action—and the effects are so good, so beautiful. We find that money is plentiful now, and we know that it will be in later years, too, and we are quickly moved into our true place where we love what we do and do what we love—without thoughts of the loss of joyful livelihood someday in the future.

We have right companionship and the ideal private and social life. We eat without fear of any food (we don't place our faith in harmfulness) because we know that all is energy, and the medicines of the past are not brought into the now. The weather is ideal wherever we go, and we live in this world for the splendid adventure it offers. Yes, all of this is true when we are on fire with Spirit and seeing only through the eyes of spiritual vision.

Let's adapt the lesson of this step for our meditation.

> *I understand now that the effects of this world are from the past and are not creative. One effect does not birth another, for everything emanates from consciousness.*
>
> *I affirm with mind and heart that no person, place, thing, condition, or situation in the external world has power over me, or has the power to create anew for me.*
>
> *I place my total dependence on Spirit within, releasing everything to the presence of God I AM, knowing that Love has met my every need, want, or desire even before they were experienced in mind and heart.*
>
> *I am as Jesus, forever one with Father-Power-Will and Mother-Substance-Love. I am a Whole Person, spiritually, mentally, emotionally, and physically. And my world reflects that Wholeness.*

L E S S O N   1 5

Trust the Ring of Protection

*Nothing can touch you but God, for God is all
there is. What is there to fear? As a Being of God,
all power is within you as protective guidance,
and around you as a shield of security.
Can you not trust omnipotence?*

In meditating on this lesson, I was reminded again that if we
fear anything in this world, we are believing in two powers,
one good and one evil. For example, we lock our cars and homes
because we believe in the power of theft and physical harm.
Many people carry guns for self-protection, believing in the
"evil" that stalks the streets, thus creating conditions to experience and prove that depravity does exist when it is nothing but an
ego-projected illusion.

But what about that misqualified energy of the collective
consciousness representing fear, anger, and hate? It is true that

people functioning primarily out of ego will attract that darkened energy, but remember that it is nothing but a thought-form that we have created. It did not come from God; therefore, there is no reality to it. When we withdraw our belief in this ego-projection as a power, knowing that there is no power apart from God, it withers and dies.

One of the most comforting and strengthening passages in the Bible is found in Isaiah 43:5: "Fear not, for I am with you." *I* am with you. Omnipotence is around you as a shield of security. Omniscience is with you as protective guidance. *What is there to fear?*

I remember the night I was about to walk down a path of hot burning coals in a firewalk. A Native American woman asked each one of us to name our most pressing fears—to talk about them and bring them to light so that their darkness could be dissolved. When I realized that there was really nothing to fear, I could feel myself growing stronger, more in tune with the Spirit within, and when I walked across the fire, I felt nothing but gentle warmth.

What are your greatest fears? Name them. Expose them, and then notice how insignificant they seem in the light. Fear cannot exist when we come to grips with Reality. As *A Course In Miracles* puts it, "There is nothing to fear. . . . The awareness that there is nothing to fear shows that somewhere in your mind, though not necessarily in a place you recognize as yet, you have remembered God, and let His strength take the place of your weakness. The instant you are willing to do this there is indeed nothing to fear."[1]

The 91st Psalm is an ideal meditation to help you replace fear with confidence. Ponder these passages with deep feeling:

He that dwelleth in the secret place of the most High shall abide under the shadow of the almighty.

I will say of the Lord, He is my refuge and my fortress; my God, in him will I trust.

Surely he shall deliver thee from the snare of the fowler, and from the noisome pestilence.

He shall cover thee with his feathers, and under his wings shalt thou trust; his truth shall be thy shield and buckler.

Thou shalt not be afraid for the terror by night; nor for the arrow that flieth by day;

Nor for the pestilence that walketh in darkness; nor for the destruction that wasteth at noonday.

A thousand shall fall at thy side, and ten thousand at thy right hand; but it shall not come nigh thee.

The promise, the absolute certainty is there, but remember the condition: to dwell in the secret place of the most High, which is nothing less than *spiritual consciousness*—the awareness, understanding, and knowledge of our Truth of Being, the God-Self I AM.

In *High Mysticism*, Emma Curtis Hopkins writes:

1. Steadfastly facing Thee, there is no evil on my pathway.
2. Steadfastly facing Thee, there is no matter with its laws.
3. Steadfastly facing Thee, there is no loss, no lack, no absence, no deprivation.
4. Steadfastly facing Thee, there is nothing to fear, for there shall be no power to hurt.
5. Steadfastly facing Thee, there is neither sin, nor sickness, nor death.[2]

Back in the 1970s, I produced a series of documentaries for the U.S. Department of Energy, and when the videos were completed, I was taken by private jet to show them to members of a special committee. On the way to the airport, I became extremely agitated. My stomach was churning and my nerves were on edge. I attributed it to an uneasy feeling about the committee's possible reaction to my work, but unknown to me at the time, Jan was experiencing the same heavy tension at home. Spirit was pressing to come through.

As I boarded the plane, I tried to release the feelings and become centered in the Presence. Jan also got busy. She went outside and sat on the patio, reaching in and up to become more attuned to Spirit—because she intuitively felt that something was going to happen to that plane.

She was right. In three separate occurrences, we almost crashed. The first was a near-collision in the air with another plane halfway to our destination. Then as we were about to land, the jet had to lift off again to avoid hitting a helicopter that suddenly plopped down on the runway. And finally, upon our return to Houston, we had to skid off the runway to avoid another plane that was landing behind us.

When I got home that night, I said, "Honey, you won't believe what happened today." And I gave her the details. She just smiled and said, "I know"—and then told me of the warning she had received and what she had done about it. *Steadfastly facing Thee, there is nothing to fear, for there shall be no power to hurt.* If we had risen high enough in consciousness, the trip would have been without the possible dangers, but even an apprehensive reach-in-and-touch-the-Presence action resulted in a safe return home.

Again, *spiritual consciousness* is the key, and with each step up Jacob's ladder we climb higher into that realm of Reality where nothing can touch us but God. But right here let's pause and remind ourselves that the God who is our ring of protection is not something apart from us, but is actually our Consciousness— not the lower nature of ego, which is only a false belief, but the Only Nature that exists as *I*. We have to do away with division and see only the one Reality.

We are not trying to move from harm to safety, from imperfection to perfection, from darkness to light. No! We *are* that safety, that perfection, that light, and this is what we must realize. There is only the fullness of God in expression as each one of us, as the mighty *I*. *I am as Jesus.*

Jesus, as Representative Being, told the appearance of evil to "Get thee hence." And when a great storm came up, he "rebuked the winds and the sea; and there was great calm." He said, "All power is given unto me in heaven and earth." He was speaking as the Complete Being we are as we embody the *all power* of the only Self.

In our spiritual awareness, let us see only the Truth, the solitary Wholeness of our Being where nothing evil, wicked, harmful, or hurtful exists. The activity of God—*spiritual consciousness*—is the only power at work. There is no other power, and let all beliefs to the contrary be uprooted and dissolved now. God is our spirit, our soul, our mind, our *everything*. So what is there to fear? Nothing! This is a benevolent universe, a world of harmony and goodwill, so let's cease projecting ignorance and false beliefs onto the screen of life.

The lesson in this step emphasizes that *"all power is within you as protective guidance, and around you as a shield of security."* It is your awareness of who and what you are that draws forth the protective guidance and the shield of security. In *Angel Energy,* I reported on numerous case histories of such rings of protection, where people were "saved" from car crashes, storms, and accidents by unseen voices and hidden hands. Why and how? These were people on the spiritual path who had realized their divine identity to some degree and had stepped into the ring of protection.

Let's consciously become one with that ring and . . .

> *"Go forward with a sense of strength, knowing that the power of your soul . . . and the protective aura which surrounds the work of the Christ can ever be relied upon."*[3]

LESSON 16

See Everything for the Good of All

✛ ✛ ✛

Whether in prayer or daily living, seek the good of all,
for God gives universally through omnipresence.

✛ ✛ ✛

This lesson immediately reminded me of Emerson's comment:
" . . . prayer as a means to effect a private end is meanness
and theft."[1]

There is only one Self, and when we seek only good for
others, we are literally drawing it to us individually. As Jesus has
said, *"Do unto others as you would have them do unto you. Thou
shalt love thy neighbor as thyself. Inasmuch as ye have done it
unto one of the least of my brethren, ye have done it unto me."*

And in the World Healing Meditation, we read: *"What is true of
me is true of everyone, for God is all and all is God. I see only the
Spirit of God in every soul. And to every man, woman, and child on
earth I say: I love you, for you are me. You are my Holy Self."*

We recognize the universal Selfhood of which we all belong, understanding that in our oneness, we cannot be exclusive in our prayers—that what we want for ourselves, we want for everyone. Whether it's a loving relationship, a healing, or financial all-sufficiency, our affirmative prayers and meditative treatments should be inclusive of the planetary family for maximum effectiveness. But this is only a part of the lesson.

The other "gem" relates to the truth that *"God gives universally through omnipresence."* Yes! "He makes his sun rise on the evil and on the good, and sends rain on the just and on the unjust." (Mt. 5:45) *Praise God from whom all blessings flow.* All blessings, all the time, without exception—an infinite, everlasting outpouring, overflowing radiation of all-inclusive supply of everything for everyone at every moment in time and space with nothing missing. There is neither reward nor punishment, only loving givingness constantly shining as completeness, and falling as nourishing wholeness for all.

Emerson also wrote that "prayer is the contemplation of the facts of life from the highest point of view. It is the soliloquy of a beholding and jubilant soul. It is the spirit of God pronouncing his works good."[2]

We contemplate the "facts from the highest point of view"—that God withholds nothing from us that is good, true, and beautiful in life. And through this joyful awareness, we see only the finished kingdom on earth.

Could it be that when our prayers seem to be unanswered, it is simply our refusal to be open and receptive to that which is ours and already given—accepting not only for ourselves but for everyone else? Let's begin now, whether in prayer or daily living, to *"seek the good of all."* We rejoice with others when they find the right life partner; we shout with joy when someone receives a financial windfall; we praise God when we hear that a healing of mind, emotions, and body has occurred.

What I want for me, I want for you! Let's keep that at the forefront of consciousness as we take the next step.

L E S S O N 1 7

Understand the Will of God

*Will is the dynamic urge to create, the purpose
and inspiration behind all things. It is singular, not
higher and lower, a power applied universally and
individually as a force for goodwill.*

*God's will and your will are one in
spiritual consciousness.*

The phrase "thy will be done" in the Lord's Prayer is a statement of resignation for many, the calling down of a power to do something that may not be what we had in mind. It's as though we're saying, "Since I can't have what I want in life, I guess I'll have to settle for what God wants." And in some cases, there's a little tinge of fear there. After all, we were brought up to believe that God punishes us for our sins, and that the will of God must contain some form of suffering and sacrifice for us. No wonder so many people live in a state of apprehension, futility, and fatalism.

And there's the opposite side of the coin. We've been told to be careful what we pray for because we might get it. In other words, "My will be done." *A Course In Miracles* states it this way:

> The very fact that the Will of God, which is what you are, is perceived as fearful, demonstrates that you are afraid of what you are. It is not, then, the Will of God of which you are afraid, but yours. . . . You do not ask only for what you want. This is because you are afraid you might receive it, and you would.[1]

But now we see that there is only one will, and how could it be otherwise? The whole universe of Cosmic Being individualized its consciousness as the Selfhood of each one of us, and nothing was left out of the individualizing process. We are the will of God. "I and God are one; all that God is, I am."

This lesson helped me understand that the burning desires of my heart born of love represented the one common will pushing on my consciousness to express. God's will is peace and joy, radiant wholeness and well-being, creative success and abundant prosperity, right relations and harmony. Is that not our will, too? There is only one will.

As I was writing my interpretation of this lesson, I received the Spring 1998 Quarterly Letter written for subscribers by my good friend, author and spiritual teacher Walter Starcke. Here is an excerpted portion from a section titled "On Demand Prayer":

> There comes a time when after days of struggling to turn things over to our Higher Consciousness, after releasing all judgment, after forgiving everyone and everything involved, if the roadblock has not been removed, the time has come for us to demand that it be. If we really believe we are one with God, then always waiting on God, always being patient, always turning it over to God, as though we have no say in the matter,

has to eventually come to an end. Passivity can be a form of doubt. Demand affirms oneness.

There comes a time when petitionary prayer is a denial of our claim to be One with God. Petitionary prayer always has an intimation of fear, always remains an acknowledgment of duality. At one point, petitionary prayer can be like programming the computer, but to get results the computer has to be turned on by demand.

Certainly, if you are operating out of ego, and if you have not exhausted all other means, the condition has not been met for your will to be on demand. But there comes a time when you must affirm your union by demanding that a situation break, a healing take place or clarification become present.

Love and then demand. Love God by affirming that God is the only power and then demand that that power, that omnipotence, be done because of your joint partnership, because you are taking responsibility for being a co-creator with God.

Your prayer should not be "thy will be done," as though there is a question or doubt, as though something apart from yourself has to be called upon. It should be, "Thy will is done, because I affirm, because I demand it."[2]

Since this book represents the steps to spiritual consciousness, let's realize the importance of the Code in this particular step. *I am as Jesus.* He said in John 11:41-42, just before the raising of Lazarus, "Father, I thank thee that thou has heard me. And I know that thou hearest me always. . . ." This was the recognition of the oneness of Spirit and soul, the one Mind and the single will, knowing that even before the call was made, the answer, the power, was given. *Thy will is done because I call it forth.* And the call here was that Lazarus be raised from the dead.

While we may not have accomplished such miracles yet, I'm sure that we can look back on our lives at those times when we spoke the word, that divine order be established or that a roadblock be removed. We were not asking God to do something that wasn't already being done. No, we were taking an action that caused a shift in our consciousness, which put us back into alignment with the one will.

I recall a time back in the 1970s when everything seemed to be in a tangled mess, and I sent forth the call to be freed from it. This demand broke the ego-grip, and the answer came quickly as an opportunity presented itself to move to another city and take an executive position with a new firm, which in time led to the forming of The Quartus Foundation and the writing of my first book, *The Superbeings*. The one will-in-action brought harmony out of chaos. "Thou shalt also decree a thing, and it shall be established unto thee; and the light shall shine upon thy ways." (Job 22:28)

Jesus asked, "What do you want me to do for you?" (Mk. 10:51) In the interplay between him and the blind man, can we see the same thing happening between our consciousness and the Divine Self within? What do you *will*? Decree that all blocks in consciousness be removed, and then go forth as the will of God to heal, multiply provisions, and bring everything in life up to the divine standard. *Be as Jesus!*

"When the light comes and you have said, 'God's will is mine,' you will see such beauty that you will know it is not of you. Out of your joy you will create beauty in His name, for your joy could no more be contained than His."[3]

A Spiritual Treatment Using the Power of Will

It is my will that every obstacle to a whole and complete life be removed.

If there is a false belief in scarcity, I decree that it be dissolved now.

If there is a lie made manifest as a physical malady, let Truth replace it now.

If an error pattern exists from judging others and is outpicturing as strained relationships, I demand that it be eliminated now.

If wrong thinking has resulted in failure, it is my will that all such thoughts be corrected now.

I am ready and willing to live a rich, whole, loving, and successful life, which is my divine birthright.

God's will is mine!

L E S S O N   **1 8**

Know That Spirit Does Not Forsake

*The sun cannot reject its rays, the sea its waves.
The All forever remains united as one, yet those with
dispirited mind may feel separated from their source
because through guilt they have forsaken Spirit as
Cause. They have given themselves to the world of
effects and have denied the only Power, loving
Forgiveness and Benevolence in action.*

Paul tells us that God has said, "I will never fail you nor forsake you." (Heb. 13:5) No, Spirit does not forsake; it is the other way around. We give up on God when we don't believe our prayers are answered—when nothing seems to work and everything appears to be in limbo—or when we are so caught up in "this world" that we forget where the power is. That's when we turn to the ego to "make things happen"—and we usually end up with a mouth full of ashes.

To interpret this lesson properly, we look once again to the truth that there is no place where we leave off and God begins. Soul and Spirit are one mind. Our conscious awareness of ourselves, life, and God is that one mind in a different vibration—in the recognition mode as distinguished from the IS mode. There is no separation; there never has been; all is God. *We are as Jesus.*

" . . . *yet those with dispirited mind can feel separated from their source because through guilt they have forsaken Spirit as Cause.*" And what is the principal reason for this? It goes back to our dependence on the external world for our happiness. If we believe that anything in the world we have created is necessary for our well-being, we are transferring our power to the world of effects. To do so is to affirm a life of feast and famine. Why? Because we have deserted Cause, our Source, and are mentally-emotionally reaching out into a world that we perceive to be filled with good and bad, pleasure and pain—and so it is.

This seeking for relief in the objective world comes from following the dictates of ego rather than the guidance of Spirit, and usually begins with feelings of guilt—a word that also denotes low self-worth, shame, and humiliation. And guilt pronounced on ourselves by ourselves about anything always results in a call, usually on an unconscious level, for punishment. Such a demand removes us from the manifestation stream of the kingdom, the Mother-substance, the all-inclusive supply—and we certainly do feel forsaken and fearful.

Guilt is an ego emotion, so the first step in healing is to *forgive*. To forgive is to give up resentment toward something or someone, and let's remember that resentment equates to anger, indignation, bitterness, hurt feelings, and vindictiveness. First, we forgive every mistake we think we've ever made, which is to forgive our ego for leading us into temptation through its misperceptions. Then we send the light of forgiveness throughout this world, and particularly to every person who comes into our mind as one who we think has hurt us in any way.

As we have discussed before, we have often prayed to God for material things, to prosper our affairs, to heal the body, or to bring us the perfect mate. And when we don't get results, we feel forsaken and doubt whether the spiritual way of life really works. It works, but our error was in asking, praying, for a change in the effect, thus disregarding the false thinking that produced the negative effect in the first place. Instead of asking God to fix our bank account and body or bring a soulmate to our door, we should ask and meditate for a healing of consciousness so that we may perceive reality rather than the error-illusion. We contemplate Spirit and let the Light dissolve the darkness. Then we accept the healing, and turn everything over to the Presence within.

I make it sound simple, and it is. The secret of life is not to change what's going on in our world, but to change our mind and our thoughts with respect to what appears to be missing, threatening, or intimidating. Ask yourself regarding any situation you are facing: How does my only Self, the Spirit of God, see this? The Light does not see darkness. Completeness does not recognize emptiness. Spirit does not see problems, only solutions. Yes, Spirit knows that in the awareness mode, needs may be perceived, but It sees those needs as already fulfilled, the question answered, the problem solved. Ask for and accept a healing of mind and emotions, forgive yourself and others, and see as Spirit sees.

What would Jesus say about that situation calling for your attention? He would tell you that the gifts of God have been given and need only be accepted. But he would point out that the gifts are not material; they are *spiritual*. The gifts of God are life, love, joy, and peace—harmony and divine order—and faith in only the absolute goodness of life. And he would remind you that it is your mind that translates these gifts into form and experience when you are focused on the truth of you, on the heavenly realm of cause within and not on the miscreated world of effects.

Don't miss this point. We created the material world with our thoughts, and we continue to create. Our minds are doing it right now depending on where we are in consciousness. Through the lower vibration of ego, we *mis*-create and suffer in and from our own fabrications, and then wonder why we're forsaken. But when we are in *spiritual consciousness*—a deep and abiding awareness, understanding, and knowledge of our true Identity—the mind is lifted to a higher frequency, where it interprets for expression only that which is good, true, and beautiful.

The woman who in faith touched Jesus' garment was healed. To the deaf man, he said, "Be open." When no fish had been caught, his instruction to the fisherman was to "let down your nets for a catch." To the man with the withered hand, he said, "Stretch out your hand." And when it was necessary to pay taxes, he said to "go to the sea and cast a hook, and take the first fish that comes up, and when you open its mouth you will find a shekel."

In every recorded miracle, Jesus represents each one of us as our Complete Self, and also the recipient of the blessing—the dispirited mind in tune with ego. Whenever a self-created effect seems to threaten us, let us remember to reach in and touch the Presence in meditation, to be open to the voice of Spirit within, to see our consciousness as the "net" for substance, the all-inclusive supply. And "hand" is the power of manifestation, so through thought we take on the power, the will, and extend it outwardly to heal the withered condition—seeing the radiation of mind-energy going before us to make all things new. Oh yes, tax time and no money. If we face such a dilemma, let's remember to go within with a listening mind, knowing that our every need is known by Spirit, and we take the first idea that comes to us. In it we will find the way to meet the situation. God meets us wherever we are in consciousness!

Let's understand that "heaven on earth"—the living of a joyous and fulfilled life—is part of the natural process. And that flow from mind to manifestation is taking place at every moment, which means that the only reason we're not living whole and complete lives is because of false beliefs. The problem is not "out there"—it's in here, in mind. But by asking Spirit to heal our mind, and then forgiving our ego and anyone who we feel has withheld our good (another false belief), we are clearing the way for that natural process. And by keeping our focus on the Presence within, we will be filling our minds with the energy of Truth, which is then expressed in the material world as *ALL*-sufficiency.

And God is able to provide you with every blessing in abundance, so that you may always have enough of everything and may provide in abundance for every good work. (2 Cor. 9:8)

LESSON 19

Understand There Is No Duality

✣   ✣   ✣

The dual nature of the universe does not exist in the True World. There is neither health nor sickness, abundance nor scarcity, peace nor conflict. God IS, the only Power, infinite and omnipresent Spirit. All else is maya, illusory appearances projected by mind, whether judged good or bad by the seer.

In Spirit, nothing is lacking, nothing is absent. Whatever is not of God does not exist. There is nothing opposed to God. Truth has no opposite; therefore, all is perfect. Spiritual consciousness knows this and does not experience duality.

✣   ✣   ✣

Think about the last movie or TV program you watched. It was filled with duality—good and bad experiences, some considered humorous, others tragic. There may have also been specific examples of the rich and poor and the well and ill. Of course. You were being shown a slice of life—human life as we know it with a view of both sides of the coin.

Now consider your animate existence on this small planet. Art imitates life. In "this world," we experience the duality of light and darkness, and all that is symbolized by the two extremes because we are constantly projecting appearances on the screen of life based on our beliefs. If we believe that we are human and subject to the trials and tribulations of such a species, so it will be unto us. We are what we believe.

In the True World, however, which is our home right here on earth, there is only the one Power—*"infinite and omnipresent Spirit."* And since this one Mind cannot know sickness, scarcity, conflict, or any of the other maladies of ego-insanity, neither does It identify with health, abundance, peace, or what we may consider the other virtues and boons of a mate-rial-physical life. Don't let that depress you. The unreality of duality, whether good or bad, can be the key to unlock the prison doors and free you from the jarring nightmare of "human" existence.

"In Spirit nothing is lacking, nothing is absent. Whatever that is not of God does not exist." We exist; therefore, we are of God and all is perfect. We are not healthy or ill, rich or poor, for we are Spirit. We are immortal beings here to show forth the glory of God, not to change the picture on the screen, but to reveal that Truth has no opposite—that there is nothing opposed to God, that there is nothing to fight against. God IS!

If we are trying to make ourselves rich or well, we are iden-tifying with a poor and sick state of mind, a power in opposition to God. There is no such power. *"Spiritual Consciousness knows this and does not experience duality."*

We Are the Kingdom of God

When we are spiritually minded, our true estate, we see ourselves as a Force Field of pure energy, the very Kingdom of God. We know ourselves to be spiritual beings living in a spiritual universe where there are no limitations, no imperfections, no incompleteness. In this state of mind, everything that becomes visible in our lives, whether form or experience, is *ideal*. There are no insufficiencies to deal with, for there is only *all*-sufficiency. There is no "health" to be concerned about, because there is only wholeness. And there is neither peace nor conflict, only universal bliss.

To be spiritually minded is to be one in mind with substance, the all-inclusive supply of Mother Love, and this consciousness-of-substance appears as every form and experience without us having to mentally project a desired condition. We don't have to make anything happen; it all comes forth into manifest form and experience through an activity of spiritual consciousness. But if we go within to Spirit for health, wealth, a relationship, or career success, we're affirming duality—that something in our world isn't right and must be fixed by Spirit. This kind of thinking is completely out of touch with Reality. *"In Spirit, nothing is lacking, nothing is absent."* And we are Spirit, in the Absolute and in expression. *I am as Jesus.*

I want to move beyond the kind of life where I am working the spiritual principles specifically to change something in the phenomenal world. I want to live a spontaneous life where wonderful things happen naturally, where all needs are met without me having to take thought about them—or even praying, meditating, or spiritually treating to grease the skids for a manifest good.

This is the way it's supposed to be, and for many of us, there have been times in our lives when this was the norm. That's when we were more spiritually in tune, and I'm sure we can remember those blissful experiences. But I don't want just periodic happy happenings, and I don't think you do either. We want a continuum of joyful living where every day is literally heaven on earth, where every activity of life is in divine order, and harmony reigns supreme. Perhaps this lesson shows us that we're already there. *There is no duality!*

If we can agree that we live in a perfect world right now—without opposites—then beliefs to the contrary will begin to be changed. There is neither health nor sickness, only pure and perfect *life*. Prosperity and scarcity do not co-exist, only *substance* which our consciousness manifests to reveal the infinity of all-inclusive supply. Can we grasp the significance of this? If we can, we will take a great leap forward in our escape from the so-called human condition.

We have been given everything, and as spiritual beings, the "everything" could only be that which is spiritual—love, life, will, creative intelligence, substance—streams of living energy representing the attributes of God. We are *consciousness*, and as we receive, accept, and embody the fullness of Spirit, we return to that original state of *knowing*. Here we know that God Is, I AM, and our world reflects back to us that Truth of Being. We rise above the world of duality into a new dimension where "the earth is the Lord's"—and every manifestation from the invisible realm into visibility is spiritual consciousness *being* that form or experience.

When we live in and as spiritual consciousness, everything in life is spontaneous, natural, automatic, and unplanned by the calculating ego-nature. All relationships are harmonized; our bodies reflect perfect life; our work is an expression of the higher vision, the divine plan; and our visible supply is a continuous manifestation of substance in accordance with whatever is needed. It is a complete life without opposition in any form.

Let's continue our climb up the ladder with this meditation:

I look upon my life, my world, through spiritual eyes now, and I see only the Truth of Being. Everyone labeled man or woman is in reality the Spirit of God made visible through mind-action. Behind this physical appearance is the one radiant Self, the Christ. It is this Presence I see in every encounter. There can be no other; God is all there is.

The Truth I see in my life, my world, is Mind in perfect manifestation, whether in structure, thing, life-form, condition, or experience. Nothing that is good and beautiful is lacking, and whatever that is not of God does not exist. I see a perfect life and a perfect world, because there is nothing opposed to God, and Truth has no opposite.

I know this now, and I am being lifted higher and higher in spiritual consciousness. I am as Jesus!

L E S S O N 20

Know the Dangers of Spiritual Pride

Spiritual pride erects a wall in the one mind as a barrier to the light of wisdom and understanding. Darkness then prevails, and there is vulnerability to conflict and duplicity, for pride leads to arrogance and pretension. It is self-glorification in its lowest form. To fulfill the goal of life, serve with humility while steadfastly holding to Truth.

When everything we know spiritually doesn't seem to work anymore and our lives appear to be bordering on the barren, let's check the gauge of spiritual pride and see if the needle has moved into the red. It can happen without us realizing it, particularly when we've been zooming along with those masterful demonstrations of the one creative power and we think we're on top of the world. We always are, in Truth, but all it takes is a bit of self-glorification to turn our world upside down.

Actually, to be spiritually proud is to be ego-centered, and the ego is the tempter. *Lead us not into temptation.* What temptation? Feelings of superiority, self-righteousness, and judgment. *"Spiritual pride erects a wall in the one mind as a barrier to the light of wisdom and understanding."* Where before there was illumination, even if only a faint glow, now there is only the darkness of confusion. When darkness prevails, it can be compared to the dark night of the soul. And it all begins when we think of ourselves as knowing something that others don't, or having a power that others have not yet discovered, or because of our spiritual quest we judge ourselves as "good"—a little more righteous than our neighbor.

Jesus said, "I of myself can do nothing"—without God I *am* nothing. And in Mark 10:17, we read: *And as he was setting out on his journey, a man ran up and knelt before him, and asked him, "Good Teacher, what must I do to inherit eternal life?" And Jesus said to him, "Why do you call me good. No one is good but God alone."*

God alone is what we are, the one and only Self, but when the ego's influence is felt, all the good is thrown out the window. There is no such thing as a "good person." The only good is God *being* that person.

Jan and I had so much success early on with metaphysical principles that we believed there was nothing we couldn't do— and we were right. The mighty *I*, the only Self, can do all things, and the more we tapped in to that Consciousness, the more the creative power was released. Then the ego began to be threatened and quietly worked its way into mind to take credit for all the marvelous accomplishments. Enter spiritual pride.

When pride comes, then comes disgrace; but with the humble is wisdom. (Prov. 11:2)

I can recall a few remarks I made to business associates who were having problems, usually in a fatherly let-me-show-you-the-way tone of voice. This was in an advertising agency back in the 1960s—I was vice president—and my advice consisted primarily of chastising the people for not using the power of their minds, with the subtle suggestion to think as I do.

The Tibetan Master, Djwhal Khul, has this to say on the subject: "The glamour of self-assurance . . . is the belief, in plain language, that the disciple regards that his point of view is entirely right. This again feeds pride and tends to make the disciple believe himself to be an authority and infallible. It is the background of the theologian."[1]

Yes, I was preaching my doctrine of metaphysics, "casting my pearls" before people who didn't know what on earth I was talking about and could care less. Later, as president of another agency, I sent a memo to the officers extolling the virtues of affirmations and suggesting we use our indwelling power to draw the appropriate clients to us. And the word around the office was that I had lost my mind. It was true that with the cloud of spiritual pride, I had lost something—that deep awareness of the Presence within—and loss attracts loss. We began losing clients and finally had to sell the agency.

Pride goes before destruction, and a haughty spirit before a fall." (Prov. 18:18)

I started over again, not only to earn a living, but to understand what the spiritual life was really all about. And I was led to study the real meaning of humility. Even with the climb back up the mountain, there were times when the ego moved into a dominant position, but at least now I knew his face and could see the immediate effect. On one occasion, after feeling rather smug about something, my ankle swelled to twice its size—no sprain or strain, just a puffing up to correspond to my way of thinking. That was about the time I decided to be Mr. Meek, a reach in the opposite direction. And I can tell you that that doesn't work either, because you come off as not being sure of yourself about anything.

The Middle Path

There is a middle path we must walk, a path between self-glorification and spiritless subservience. *"To fulfill the goal of life serve with humility while steadfastly holding to Truth."* I discussed humility in my book *Living a Life of Joy*:

> Many of us may equate humility with weakness, whereas just the opposite is true. Just look at the antonyms of humility: pride, arrogance, rudeness, vanity, pretentiousness, pomposity, and boastfulness. A person known for these characteristics is indeed weak.
>
> True humility means being open and receptive to new ideas. It is being unpretentious. It is the consciousness of consent, a willingness to be shown the higher path through a surrender of the (ego). With humility our true worthiness begins to shine as the noonday sun. Without it a form of rigidity may set in, which becomes another experience to work through.[2]

As we walk the middle path, we do so with an open mind and heart, knowing that the wisdom and understanding that we have—and which will increase even more—is from the Mind of God and not the arrogance of ego. We are centered in Spirit and find our strength there. We don't depend on the external world for our good; we see everything for the good of all; we understand the will of God; and we know that Spirit could never forsake us. When it is necessary to keep our mouths shut, we will do so, and when it is appropriate for us to speak our truth, we will know that it is Truth itself speaking, and we shall not be fearful in expressing ourselves.

On the middle path, we are true to our Selves, the great and grand Self that we are. "It is easy to distinguish grandeur from grandiosity, because love is returned and pride is not. Pride will not produce miracles, and will therefore deprive you of the true witnesses to your reality."[3] *A Course In Miracles* is right. Total Self-reliance is based on love where pride is not, and does indeed produce the miracles.

To firm our position on this step up the ladder, let's work with this meditative treatment:

> *I agree from this moment on to do my very best to keep my mind on the Presence I AM, to feel love and joy, to think loving thoughts toward all, and to always act from a sense of inward direction.*
>
> *To accomplish this, I again release all fears, resentment, condemnation, and unforgiveness. I surrender all past mistakes and errors in judgment, and I empty out all false pride and ego-centered emotions.*
>
> *Everything in my consciousness that could possibly hold me in bondage I now cast upon the Christ within to be dissolved. I now choose to live under grace, in spiritual consciousness. And I see and know this consciousness to be the perfect harmonizing influence in all relationships, the perfect adjustment in all situations, the perfect release from all entanglements, the perfect fulfillment in my life.*
>
> *I now go forth in faith, putting my trust in Christ as my consciousness, and living each moment with a heart overflowing with gratitude, love, and joy.*

LESSON 21

Be Yourself

Self-image must be the awareness of your Holiness, for That is all you are, yet your uniqueness as an Individual comes from many lifetimes of experiences, all of which makes you indispensable in the cosmic process. Do not imitate others or strive to be someone you are not. Value the distinctive contribution you came to make to this world. Know your worth. Be yourself.

I thought about the men and women who come to the Quartus gatherings and pondered the piece of the cosmic puzzle that each one carries in their self-identity. And you, reading this book—have you considered that you are different from anyone else in the whole world, both sides of the veil included? With all your adventures, undertakings, journeys, and experiences in the role-playing of all types of characters on the stage of many lives, no one has had the same kind of universal "seasoning" that you have.

In a very mystical experience in the light, my mother was told by audible voices from unseen beings that Jan and I had walked many lands, were exposed to a great variety of cultures, spoke different languages, and experienced suffering and joy, despair and hopefulness, failure and success—the full range of human emotions and endurance—to bring us to where we are now and to prepare us for our current assignment. The same could be said about you. You came into this life with your piece of the puzzle, and this world would not be complete without you and your contribution to the whole cosmic process. There's no one like you anywhere. And in God's scheme of things, that's perfect, because you can use your particular unmatched key to open the lock that was assigned to you just prior to this incarnation. Yes, you do have a mission, and you can fulfill it only by being yourself.

"Self-image must be the awareness of your Holiness"—and we're deepening that awareness through these steps—*"yet your uniqueness as an individual comes from many lifetimes of experiences."* Over eons, we have honed our consciousness to include our talents and abilities, our particular viewpoints on life, and our way of expressing ourselves. We have chosen a great variety of planetary energies to incarnate in, each time with a different sun sign (personality expression), rising sign (the purpose of Spirit), and moon (representing our past). There's no telling how many times we have gone through the entire zodiac, which means that we have subjected ourselves to a vast array of conditioning energies.

And then consider the fact that we choose our parents in each incarnation—or consent to them playing the role—which subjects us to their energy fields and the governing forces at play in their consciousness. No wonder there are no two of us alike.

You say, "But I'm just me." That's the point. You are *you*! And while you may not know at this time the exact meaning of your thread that has been woven into the universal fabric and how it makes the kingdom complete, you can be sure that Spirit knows. You *will* have the opportunity to fulfill your mission, and there is no greater or lesser mission, so don't think in terms of insignificance.

Isn't this really the heart of the Code? As I wrote in the Introduction:

> He is saying, "I was physical, I had a personality, I used my mind, and I expressed my feelings—all in unison as the Spirit of God, which all of you are. So stand strong as a complete person, apologizing not for wearing a coat of skin or for being the sum-total of your experiences. The world needs you as you are, and your false beliefs will be corrected as you take all of you into spiritual consciousness."

Let's not try to be something or someone we're not. I am me and you are you, and with every step we take into spiritual consciousness, the error thoughts are burned away. In the meantime, we accept ourselves as we are at this moment. I know I'm not the same person I was a year ago, or perhaps even a month ago. We are all growing up, up, and until we reach our Destination, let's just be ourselves.

An interview with someone usually begins with "Tell me about yourself." And we usually try to cover the positive ground—hit only the high spots—and keep that part of ourselves hidden that may seem unconventional, strange, or offbeat. Even in our interactions with people, we may attempt to show only our "good" side as we intuit what *their* interpretation of good and bad may be. But remember . . .

You are consciousness, therefore you have a personality, as I do, which is an expression of your uniqueness. Do not deny or condemn it or the world will lose a particular flavor in the great miscellany of life.

It all gets back to being true to ourselves, and not trying to always please others by adhering to their rigid expectations. Jan and I are blessed with friends who are a bit eccentric and play their flavorful roles totally in character. They are outlandishly theatrical, delightfully earthy, and wildly imaginative in their perspectives on life. We love their integrity because they are always who they are.

And finally, *"Know your worth. Be yourself."* Knowing your worth and being yourself go hand in hand. In *Living a Life of Joy,* I wrote: "I recognize my true worth and do not wish to be something other than what I am. God is not complete without me, which means that who I am is the most important part of the universe at the point where I am. I meditate deeply on this for greater understanding."[1]

Worthiness is made up of three vital attributes. The first one is innocence, meaning guiltless and blameless. The second is humility, and the third is reverence for life and all that is involved in it. The three united in consciousness bring us to a state of worthiness.

A Meditation

God expressed Itself as me, and I eternally live in God, with God, as the Spirit of God. The fullness of the Godhead dwells in me and expresses through me as every good and perfect thing. I am a channel for positive change in this world.

I recognize my value as an individual being living on earth at this time. As the very worthiness of God, I am part of the Grand Plan of continuing creation, and my contribution to this world is vitally important in the divine scheme of things.

Poised, powerful, and peaceful, I do my part with love and joy. I am guiltless, open and receptive to right action, and devoted to my purpose in life. Everything I do is meaningful and worthwhile. I am deserving because I know who I am.

Live Only As Spiritual Consciousness

Play your role in life as yourself with the relish and passion of the moment, yet do not wander in mind from the Truth that you are a spiritual being, a single Identity ever perfect and complete.

You were not created as a separate being, for God does not know other than Itself. God is Consciousness, and it is only Consciousness that is considered individually.

You have no mind of your own, for there is only one Mind; no mortality exists, no separate being— only the One which you are. All is Spirit.

The cup of spiritual awareness is ever filled by Spirit, until awareness itself dissolves into knowing through complete abandonment to the one Being.

Where do most people live in and as consciousness? Some think of themselves primarily as a body—they are *body* conscious—and will try every external remedy available to make themselves feel better, younger, more energetic and vital. Many are more emotionally based and identify with a range of reactive feelings and sensations, while others combine thinking and feeling as the predominant consciousness.

Until our identity is transferred to Spirit, our only Self, while continuing to live *with the relish and passion of the moment*, we are not living the Truth of our Being, and our lives will be incomplete.

Through the steps we have covered thus far, the central theme has been the truth of our single Identity. God is all there is. If it is not of God, it does not exist. We are of God, and it is impossible for there to be anything unlike God in, through, and as us. There is only Spirit, in the Absolute and in Self-awareness—one Mind operating on different vibrations. We are that Spirit, that Mind; there is no other.

We can't be separate from God because God does not break Itself into parts. *All* of God is where we are, what we are. The sense of "human" is but an ego thought, a false belief. When we mistakenly perceived ourselves as a body and as something other than the Spirit of God, the effect was similar to a funnel-shaped waterspout in the ocean—a whirlwind that sucked the very Truth from our minds, leaving us in a void to be filled by the fearfully created ego. But now we are dissolving that vortex of lies and are returning to the still waters of the kingdom, where our only Self resides in peace and joy.

When our mind is focused on Self-Reality—not just "within" but as the *all* of us —we feel the warmth entering our heart, the recognition of the Presence in our thoughts, and the touch of Spirit all around us. *"The cup of spiritual awareness is ever filled by Spirit, until awareness itself dissolves into knowing through complete abandonment to the one Being."* We become that which we contemplate.

> *"Spirit am I, a holy Son of God,*
> *Free of all limits, safe and healed and whole,*
> *Free to forgive, and free to save the world."*[1]

> *"I am the holy Son of God Himself.*
> *I cannot suffer, cannot be in pain;*
> *I cannot suffer loss, nor fail to do*
> *All that salvation asks."*[2]

God, Consciousness, is our only Self, our only *I,* our only Existence, our All in All, and we must live as this Truth. *I am God being Me. I am as Jesus.*

In one of the old Sacred Academies, the students were drilled day and night in the truth of their divine identity, and they were given heavy chains to hang around their necks to serve as a constant reminder. I don't know if that worked or not. The students probably became so chain-conscious that the awareness of Spirit was dimmed. In my experience, and Jan's, we have found that awareness deepens with every spiritual activity. The books, tapes, and workshops are starting points, and meditation is the fertilizer that makes the seed-thoughts grow into realizations. But we have found that the real progress takes place when we do our very best to keep the dial set on Spirit moment by moment, hour by hour, day by day. We do this mostly through feelings of gratitude—a continuous offering of "Thank you" for seen and unseen blessings, being receptive to the overflowing love from within, and listening for that inner voice of revelation. We also "practice the Presence" by remembering omniscience—the infinite Knowingness of Spirit—and omnipotence, the one and only Power at work in our lives.

It was also made very clear to me one morning in meditation

that spiritual consciousness means to love *who* we are—the Lord-Self occupying the only space *where* we are—with total adoration. I nodded in agreement, and the inner voice said:

> *"Do not pass this by until you understand its meaning. There must be a complete surrender to the one Spirit, a relinquishing of everything in absolute reverence for the majesty of the One. To love your Lord with all of mind and heart is to exalt, adore your Self with all of your being, as though in the very presence of God, which you are. This does not imply a dual nature. It is looking into the mirror of Mind to see your Self. It is the ray worshiping the sun, the expression honoring the Word."*

It was then that I fully understood what "complete abandonment to Spirit" really meant. It is through this intense passion, love, and devotion directed inwardly toward the Magnificent Self we are that dissolves the awareness into knowing.

Pause for a moment now, look within, and adore your Holy Self as you never have before. Give yourself fully to the Presence with all your love in mind and heart, then be still, listen, and feel the response. This could be a life-changing experience right at this moment. And let us not forget that everyone is the Spirit of God, the Christ, and that we should love and honor that neighbor as our Self.

Yes, living in spiritual consciousness requires discipline, but it is certainly worth the effort because after a time we realize that the ego is no longer in control and that Spirit is expressing in and through and as us—at least to the extent of our awareness, understanding, and knowledge of Spirit. Countless individuals have made the commitment and are now crossing the bridge to that Promised Land, as shown by these letters I've received:

"I can't believe how lost in the dark I was. Instead of a broken-down, hateful, and lonely world, now I see a perfect, lovely, and beautiful world. I can't explain the joy I've experienced now that I know who I really am, and the purpose behind all suffering. Now my life has meaning, and instead of wandering aimlessly, there's a narrow path lighted up for me."

"I had the conscious realization that I had attained enlightenment when I became 40 years old. . . . I felt the weight of the world lifted from my shoulders. Life was no longer a burden of suffering, sorrow, or depression. I felt ten years younger, as I had the feeling that I had found the fountain of youth. I sensed a beautiful place of peace and wholeness."

"I went out in the car and drove around. Many times when I do this, and the conscious mind is busily engaged in driving, thoughts or intuitive things come to me. But I marked yesterday down on my calendar because it was the most eventful message I have ever received in my life. I heard a different voice, one that I have not heard before. It was so profound that I had to stop the car. I was told enough to fill volumes of books in just a few fleeting seconds. I was shown how my whole life so far has led up to this point, what my true function in this life is, and how the future will be for me if I do this work."

"I know now that people make a terrible error when they deny their own divinity, when they believe that they cannot perform the greatest of miracles for the benefit of all living things. If necessary, one person alone could transform the entire planet Earth, simply because each of us is blessed with Divine Power, Divine Wisdom, and above all, Divine Love."

"For many years I have been excited to be alive at this time, but never have I felt more fulfilled than now. Nature sings the message of balance to me at a louder decibel each day. In Nature I am learning my true identity, my true reason for living, and each and every day my life has less separation. 'Rejoice! The Kingdom of Heaven is at hand.'"

"The light is brighter each day, and illusion fades in the light like dreams of the night before. As I lie in bed and give all to Spirit, I awake in the morning and the day is truly new. As if by magic, the cares of yesterday have no power to steal my joy. And as I give myself to Spirit, I, too, disappear, and lo, there is only God. Now there is wholeness, oneness, and joy, for the concealing curtain has been swept aside, and the soul is flooded with light. Where once I was, now God is."

The experience of one can be the experience of all, tailored to the particular consciousness of each individual. In addition to understanding the lessons, begin now to equate God, the Truth of you, with all that you hear, feel, and see. This will expand your spiritual awareness even more and quicken the moment of realization.

Every time you hear a bird sing, *think of God*, then say, "I am That I AM, none other but that One."

Whenever you feel a soft breeze, *think of God*, then say, "God is all there is . . . *I* am the gentle wind, for *I* am all there is."

When the rays of the sun shine on you, *think of God*, then say, "*I* am omnipresent as the shining sun. My rays are warm and soothing."

Glancing at a flower, *think of God*, then say, "*I* am expressing as all that is good, true, and beautiful in life, for there is only one life, one presence, that which I AM."

When you walk, *think of God*, then say, "*I* am walking the body. *I* am the power of animation. There is no other power."

Encountering another person, *think of God*, then nod and speak silently, "Thou are the Spirit of the living God, the Holy Self I AM. When I see Thee, I see Me."

Whenever you have that intuitive feeling of knowing, that flash of revelation, *think of God*, then say, "*I* speak and *I* listen, for there is only one Voice speaking to Itself. All is God."

This is what spiritual consciousness is all about, where every question is answered and every so-called problem is solved, and we find ourselves living in the divine state of total fulfillment. It is *spiritual consciousness* that does the work!

A Meditation from the Lesson

I live with the relish and passion of the moment, yet I do not wander in mind from the Truth that I am a spiritual being, a single Identity ever perfect and complete.

I was not created as a separate being, for God does not know other than Itself. God is Consciousness, and it is only Consciousness that expresses individually. I am Consciousness.

I have no mind of my own, for there is only one Mind; no mortality exists, no separate beings, only the One which I am. All is Spirit.

Through love and adoration I have given myself completely to Spirit, and the awareness of Self is fading into the supreme, absolute knowing of Who I am.

I live only as spiritual consciousness.

LESSON 23

See the Paranormal As Normal

Normal is the ordinary, the expected, yet in spiritual consciousness one may see, feel, and experience that which is beyond the range of the normal, thus offering a heightened view of life. Do not fear this, but accept it as etheric vision into the subjective realm behind the physical.

It would not surprise me if a large percentage of you have had highly unusual experiences that could not be explained initially, but were later considered as part and parcel of your spiritual life. I know that Jan and I certainly have, and what we've learned over the years is that seeing *"beyond the range of the usual"* is a gift to enable us all to prove that we are more than "human," that nothing is impossible, and to demonstrate to us the existence of multiple worlds and dimensions—that "life" is much more than we ever perceived it to be.

For example, we have seen globes of pulsating light in our bedroom at night, and once, as they suddenly disappeared, Jan said, "Oh, don't go." And they instantly reappeared to dance around the room. What were they? We considered them to be angel energy. And those of you who have read my book by the same term, *Angel Energy*, know about the large being of light that appeared in our bedroom in the summer of 1985. And, yes, the experience did frighten me. Perhaps it wouldn't have if I had known then to *"not fear this but accept it as etheric vision."*

Time has also seemed to work for us, and two particular occasions come to mind. The first was the considerable delay of a flight from Los Angeles, which meant that we would miss our connection in Dallas and not be home when expected. Somehow time was compressed, stood still, enabling us to arrive home on schedule. Then we were on the *Geraldo Rivera* show in December 1997 to talk about the angels that appeared in our bedroom at the time of Jan's near-death experience. We had a great time, but the taping was delayed and we knew we would miss our flight. Stuck in traffic in Manhattan, I looked at my watch, and so did Jan. No way we could make it. When we arrived at the airport, our watches were still on the hour and minute hands as before. Time had literally stopped.

"Albert Einstein, the father of modern physics, posited that there is no absolute time. Rather, he said, time changes with the motion of a particular observer. We treat time as though it was linear, one thing leading to another. But Einstein showed that past, present, and future need have no fixed status."[1]

Our friend Jean in Little Rock certainly views the paranormal as normal after her experience. She was riding as a passenger in an automobile when (the driver) approached a green light at a busy intersection and proceeded through it just as another car ran the red light. Jean wrote: "A split second before the impending crash, we seemed to move into a higher vibrational state, and the two cars literally drove through each other—like walking through a wall. I can still see that car coming right at us, yet we and the cars were untouched."

All is energy. Spiritual consciousness knows this and is able to change the vibration in a situation for the good of all. Look at what happened to Jesus in Luke 4:27-30 when the people "rose up and put him out of the city, and led him to the brow of the hill on which their city was built, that they might throw him down headlong. But passing through the midst of them he went away." That "higher vibrational" state is available to all of us when we are in tune with Truth.

In Chapter 4, reference was made to out-of-body experiences (OBEs). Right after my stepfather died in the early '70s, I left my body to visit him on the other side, and I was directed to a hospital. When I inquired about him, I was told that it was too early to visit, to come back at another time. That OBE wasn't planned; it was a totally spontaneous happening. A few years later, I was reading in bed one night and Jan was asleep. Out of the corner of my eye, I caught her leaving the body, floating across me and exiting through the wall. I thought, *She's getting out ahead of me,* and I promptly tried to catch her. It didn't work that time, but since then we have found that out-of-body travels are not that difficult.

Jan also has the gift of seeing with the inner eye. It doesn't happen all the time, but frequently she can see as well with her eyes closed as when they're open. Even in a never-before-seen environment, she can close her eyes and describe every detail. It would appear that her third-eye center has been awakened. Perhaps, as we climb the spiritual ladder in consciousness, the etheric is energized to open the door to the spiritual realms outside and beyond the ordinary sensory apparatus. That's when we begin to see energy behind forms and gain a greater understanding of the nonphysical universe.

As interesting as all this may be, let's remember that mystical experiences are not the objective of spiritual consciousness.

They are only by-products, so let's don't put the cart before the horse again. Our goal in life is to be the Whole Person we were created to be, and to experience Reality by living on a higher frequency in consciousness. Then, as the experiences come, we will be properly equipped mentally and emotionally to appreciate them for what they are—an understanding of, or glimpses into, *"the subjective realm behind the physical."*

A Course in Miracles says:

> There are, of course, no "unnatural" powers, and it is obviously merely an appeal to magic to make up a power that does not exist. It is equally obvious, however, that each individual has many abilities of which he is unaware. As his awareness increases, he may well develop abilities that seem quite startling to him. Yet nothing he can do can compare even in the slightest with the glorious surprise of remembering Who he is.[2]

LESSON 24

See No Separation
Between Planes
of Existence

✛ ✛ ✛

*In God there is only oneness, in heaven and earth as abodes,
and heaven in earth as complete happiness, but here let us
contemplate the former. There is no separation between the
invisible universe of many worlds and the visible world.
They are united as the depths and shallows of the sea, the
heat and soft light of the sun. Therein lies the truth of
everlasting life and the many mansions.*

*All dimensional passageways are clear, unbounded,
with great activity through the open doors toward the
plane on which you find yourself. Herein is the
confirmation of the coming transformation on earth.*

✛ ✛ ✛

We have thought of heaven and earth as two separate geographical places—one where we live in physical bodies, the other our dwelling place after we drop the body. And, we have considered "heaven on earth" to mean the sheer bliss of living in this material world when in a state of spiritual consciousness. Now we understand that heaven and earth as homes are one, interpenetrating, and that the earthly paradise we have been seeking is not to come but already is. This latter point was not emphasized in the lesson, but let's give it a quick look.

Jesus said, "The kingdom of heaven is at hand," which means that it is here now. Of course. Think of *omnipresence, omniscience,* and *omnipotence*—the one Presence, Mind, and Power. How could it be otherwise? It is through spiritual consciousness that we experience heaven and earth as one, as the bliss of living spiritually on the material plane. God sees us as perfect and so we are. In spiritual consciousness, we see that nothing needs to be healed; we are already whole and complete. Nothing needs to be prospered because we are the focal point of infinite substance-love, which is eternally expressing as the riches of the universe.

And to that universe we hold up Completeness. We say, *Look at Me! I have no wants or needs because I have everything, and nothing can be added or taken away. I am the totality of all that God is, now and forever more.* And the universe reflects back to us that which we are, and we see only shining perfection in every activity of life wherever we are, wherever we go.

Now let's return to the oneness of our abodes, physical and nonphysical, interpenetrating.

Jan wrote in her book, *The Other Side of Death*:

> The Great Beyond is not out or up, but *in*—in you and me and everyone else—right where we are at this moment. In our three-dimensional way of thinking this may be difficult to grasp, but the other side of death is simply another dimension,

and the door to that dimension is within our individual energy fields. It is a "secret place"—a cosmic longitude and latitude in deep inner consciousness—an energy vortex through which we pass to the world of heaven, a world closer than breathing. Now we can understand why those who have passed over can still seem to be so close to us. They are.[1]

In referring to her near-death experience, Jan asks:

What has this well-beaten path of comings-and-goings done to that energy vortex within each one of us that represents the door, or veil, between the two worlds? Has the collective density been reduced to such an extent that it is no longer a substantial barrier? In my opinion the answer is yes. I believe that there is now a permanent rip in the curtain, enabling those on the other side to enter the physical world at will.[2]

Scientists who have studied near-death experiences conclude that the world beyond is a *frequency world*—that is, on a higher frequency than the material world but not separate from this plane of existence, and can be accessed through a *change in consciousness.* Those who have gone before us have never left. They are right where we are, aware of neither time nor space, simply in conscious existence on other frequencies of consciousness—the frequencies of the nonphysical world. *"There is no separation between the invisible universe of many worlds and the visible world."*

When my mother would tell me about the many visits that my father has made from "beyond the veil," I never thought about him making a long journey through outer space, or coming back through some form of tunnel. No, my father appeared from *inner space* when my mother needed help, in each case stepping forth as a full-bodied figure.

I have written about the Chinese man and older woman who

stood behind me and Jan during our early workshops, invisible to us but seen by different people in the audience who described the same appearance and clothing. Later I wrote, "They probably became visible to others so that their appearance could be relayed to us, thus negating any spiritual pride over our newfound ability to convey Truth ideas. We were not in this alone; we had holy helpers."[3] Years later I realized how true this was when three people suddenly materialized in our living room to offer me encouragement on my mission in this life—and then left in an equally dramatic fashion. I was so touched that tears flowed for hours.

We have received letters from people all over the country telling about visits from other worlds. I thought this one was particularly fascinating:

> "*Several years ago I was in the midst of a very troubling situation at work. I felt no support from peers during a bad time with my supervisors, and was completely demoralized and probably depressed, in a clinical definition of the term. I was having suicidal thoughts and was not able to even fathom the idea of other options— killing myself seemed to be the only way out from my deep sadness.*
>
> "*Well, I was sitting in a restaurant one afternoon, just staring off into space after giving my order, when a woman, a stranger, slid into the seat opposite me in my booth. She looked me straight in the eye and said, 'Do not commit suicide.' She talked to me a little while longer, and I don't remember the exact words, just that the words were along the same line. I was speechless. I just nodded agreement, then when she left I never gave another thought to suicide.*"[4]

In *Hello from Heaven,* by Bill Guggenheim and Judy Guggenheim, the authors report on interviews with 2,000 people who believe they have been contacted by a loved one who has died. Here is one case:

Virginia is a nurse in Massachusetts. She was immediately relieved when her 17-year-old daughter, Erica, came back to her after dying in an automobile accident:

"Almost a year later, I woke up one night and Erica was standing at the end of the bed. She looked at me and seemed to be in a happy mood. She appeared to be in perfect health with no injuries or anything.

"It was Erica, in person! She seemed alive and well! She was very vivid. She had on a navy blue skirt and sweater that she used to wear a lot. She seemed solid and looked very, very peaceful.

"Erica had a slight smile and said, 'I'm fine, Mom. I'm all right. Don't worry about me.' It only lasted about twenty seconds or so, and then she suddenly disappeared. A peace came over me at that moment, and I went right back to sleep."[5]

This certainly does give us proof of everlasting life, that there is no such thing as death. And when Jan was on the other side, she was shown various levels (frequencies?), thus supporting the idea of the many mansions. When we leave this plane, we take our consciousness with us, and we go to the particular level or frequency that corresponds to our state of consciousness.

When one slips back through the veil, he or she does not always appear physical. Other than the large being of light who walked into our bedroom, we have sensed the presence of others in our home many times, and we have seen what the Guggenheims call "partial appearances"—a transparent mist or a brilliant light. And on two occasions, spiritual psychics have been amazed by the number of entities who were "hanging around." In all probability, they would say the same thing about your home.

Now why is it necessary for us to know that there is no separation between planes of existence, other than the truth of everlasting life? In meditating on this concept, I heard the inner voice say, "For peace on earth"—and I was shown again the second paragraph of this lesson: *"All dimensional passageways are clear, unbounded, with great activity through the open doors toward the plane on which you find yourself. Herein is the confirmation of the coming transformation on earth."*

I thought for a moment, feeling that it was our obligation—the ones in physical form—to clean up our mess by rising into spiritual consciousness. And then I asked if people from other dimensions were really coming to assist us. The answer: "The movement began years ago, both unseen and seen."

I remembered the voice I heard in September 1984 that said it was time for me to begin a period of world service, which led to the establishment of World Healing Day on December 31, 1986. And who gathered the more than 500 million people together at one moment in time without publicity or advance media coverage? It was not "humanly" possible. I also thought about the feather that mysteriously appeared in my study on July 14, 1985—after I had written Chapter 1 in *Practical Spirituality* about changing the mass and velocity of the world's negative energy from a rock to a feather.

The Harmonic Convergence in August 1987 came to mind, and the multitude of peace events that have occurred over the years. I recalled the "chance encounters" with total strangers who said something that inspired me to think globally for the good of all, the unknown men and women in dreams who conveyed particular messages of love and peace, and the small key that materialized in my car following a meeting to discuss World Healing Days in 1998 and 1999.

We are all being influenced to participate in this great revolution of mind and heart to reveal lasting peace on earth. And this lesson implies that there are legions of men and women from beyond the veil who are coming through the dimensional passageways, adding their spiritual consciousness to serve in whatever capacity necessary for the dawning of the new world. And they are seeking those with an awakening consciousness—the Path Walkers with whom they can cooperate and communicate.

Isn't it also possible that there is another reason for this "well-beaten path," to use Jan's words? That through their sheer weight of *spiritual* consciousness, those coming through will have an impact on the collective mind quicker than we could alone? I think so.

In *Emissary of Light,* author James F. Twyman visited war-torn Bosnia and Croatia and discovered a mythical community known as the Emissaries of Light. And in a conversation with a Teacher, James was told, "Thousands of people just like you will take this step and become examples for the world. You will do this by existing outside the world and within it at the same time. Humanity will see the way you exist and learn from your example." And when James asks, "What is the Door to Eternity?" he is told, "It is an entryway to truth that has been right in front of you all along. As a human being, you exist in a three-dimensional universe. And yet there are other dimensions of which you are completely unaware but which you have the ability to access."

Later, the Teacher says, "Help them understand how holy they are, that they are all Emissaries of Light. Humanity has taken an incredible step, and with that step comes new responsibility. Help them put down their toys and accept peace where it really is—within. I am always with you, Jimmy. Never forget that."

Then, as James states it, "Suddenly he was gone. The light vanished, and I was sitting at the top of the hill alone."[6]

Obviously the Emissaries are part of that *"great activity through the open doors toward the plane on which you find yourself."* Many have arrived and more are coming. We are not alone in this great quest.

And so we take the steps to join them in spiritual consciousness, and enthusiastically consent to be a part of the team coming together from both sides of the veil to reveal the Divine Plan on earth.

LESSON 25

See Only Peace

✥ ✥ ✥

*The Code that I have freely given is spiritual con-
sciousness. I am the Code; I am spiritual consciousness. When you have one, you have the other. When
I said to be me, I was saying to be as me, to follow
me in spiritual consciousness by recognizing
that all that I am, you are.*

*The Code is spiritual law, which is the only
assurance of peace and harmony, whether in the
family or among nations. As the world moves toward
the end and a new beginning, it will continue to
mirror the illusion of darkness as the dominant force.
Pray not to change the course of events or the cause
of conflict will not be revealed, nor display reactive
interference, for life must be played as projected
by the collective mind, otherwise the just
end will only be delayed.*

*Collective thoughts shape and propel energy into
self-fulfilling prophecies. With each millennium,
the fear grows because of the expanded collective.
Yet be not apprehensive, for the errors will be*

corrected with the awakening of the collective through the activity of the Christ.

Peace is denied to all who encroach in the name of national security, to those who violate spiritual principles in the name of religion, to those whose cause is considered more moral or just than another, to those who serve only for selfish interests, for they will remain in the shadows.

Peace is granted by law of consciousness to those who seek and find the Truth. Truth, which is the universal Christ, reveals that there is no law to sustain the darkness, no power in evil, no reality to human consciousness with its emphasis on self-preservation. This is the Code. I am the Code, yet the Code as spiritual consciousness encompasses all thought processes relating to the one God, and not just a religion with which I am identified.

The family environment, the communities, the nations, the world can only be saved through spiritual consciousness—not through verbal persuasion, religious conversion, theological decrees, political aggrandizement, or any other human endeavor. Spiritual consciousness does not speak, does not pray for one side or another, does not dictate a course of action for good to vanquish evil. Spiritual consciousness does nothing but release the Christ to do the healing work in the collective life of the family, the community, the nation, the world. And the impulses of love and goodwill are felt by all.

To fully understand the Code, you must look to the ultimate Truth: Thou art the Christ. It was said that God so loved the world that he gave his only Son, that the world might be saved through him. Every man, woman, and child is this only Son, the Christ, the visible expression of the invisible God. And it is through the Christ that peace will come to earth.

It is through spiritual consciousness, Christ consciousness, that ignorance will be removed; in the united Selfhood, superstition is dissolved. Be the Mind through which the light shines to reveal Reality.
See only peace.

In this lengthy and detailed lesson, we are asked to equate the Code with Jesus and spiritual consciousness, and to recognize that all he is, we are. Then we are given an insight into the future with the collective darkness being the dominant force, followed by the statement: *"Pray not to change the course of events or the cause of conflict will not be revealed, nor display reactive interference, for life must be played as projected by the collective mind, otherwise the just end will only be delayed."* And we are told not to be apprehensive during this process, *"for the errors will be corrected."*

To me, this meant that the world is going to move along as before, only with a much more furied pace of religious intolerance, so-called moral crusades, posturing nationalism, corporate greed, and heightened selfish interests. Those in tune with self-fulfilling prophecies will see this as an opportunity for accelerated religious proselytizing, theological edicts, and political grandstanding. And what will our role be in the scheme of things? Nothing from the "human" standpoint. *"Spiritual consciousness does nothing but release the Christ to do the healing work . . . and the impulses of love and goodwill are felt by all."*

We let "human" nature as projected by the ego play itself out on the stage of life, without any emotional interference and regardless of how critical it appears. Understand that every prop in the dramatic production of "this world" must be relied on by the cast, because that is where their consciousness is. And for those operating out of ego-nature, the problems must be solved on the level of consciousness where they originated—until there is sufficient light to dispel the darkness.

On the day of the final review of this chapter, the newspaper is full of reports on the NATO bombing of Serbia, the Serbian campaign against ethnic Albanians in Kosovo, political turmoil in Paraguay, the Israeli-Palestine conflict, computer virus attacks, the rise of the neo-Nazi movement in Russia, and the political chaos in America. And who knows what we may read and see in the months ahead. According to the lesson, each situation and development will continue on course toward its just end—the conflicts to be solved within the consciousness that created them, or until the spiritual awakening of the collective mind.

And while the play continues, we begin to take our stand. We give up our false identities as humans and take on the full power of spiritual consciousness, not praying for one side or another, not dictating a course of action for good to vanquish evil, but to let the Light of Christ be released to do its mighty work. We begin as one individual, and then we unite in mind and heart with another, and then another, and still another—reaching out to bond with those who know they are the visible expressions of the invisible God.

Let's begin now, this day—in our homes, wherever we are— to go within and up to that highest frequency in consciousness, release the Light, Love, and Energy of Spirit, and see only peace in this world. And then at noon Greenwich time on December 31, 2000, the actual last day of this millennium, we will come together in one moment in time for the global mind-link. And remember, those from other dimensions are coming in to assist in the healing of the world. *"The movement began years ago, both unseen and seen."*

As we reach this step, we are more aware than we've ever been of our spiritual Identity. We understand the dynamics of Christhood and how the activity of Christ from the very core of our being goes forth to dissolve the human sense and positively influence the leaders of every government, religion, institution, and business—and the population of the world itself.

In our silence of *knowing*, the Word is spoken through us, and the Power is let out into the world—into the collective consciousness—and the great shift begins. Self-fulfilling prophecies are not realized, and the illusions are dispelled to reveal spiritual Reality—the one world of peace, love, and joy. It is the spiritual awakening of the collective through the activity of the Christ.

And we behold the true meaning of The Second Coming.

The final communication of the Jesus Code came, as it began, in a dream. I was shown a large ball nearly as tall as I was, and a male voice told me to grab the ball. As I tried to do so, it moved away. I began chasing the ball and it continued to elude my grasp.

Then he said, "To catch the ball, you must *become* the ball."

Perplexed, I asked how to do this.

"Find the point of contact within your mind that corresponds to the object of the ball. *See* within. *Feel* within. Now slowly walk into that which you are seeing and feeling and *become* the ball."

I followed the instruction, and after several attempts, I suddenly was the ball and the ball was me, in complete oneness.

And he said, "This is the secret of prayer."

"But I wasn't praying," I said.

"That is the secret of the Code."

I woke up and thought about the dream. That which we chase runs from us, whether health, wealth, success, or right relations. To be as Jesus means to be still and *become* that which we seek, that which we already are and have in the completeness of our being. Then everything we desire through our vision of the ideal life will literally chase us. The ball in the dream represented each and every aspect of the finished kingdom on earth, the wholeness of life where every aspiration is already fully manifest. We are to see and feel the energy of peace, joy, abundance, wholeness, success, and loving relationships. We are to see and feel it, step into it, and become it. And when we do, our concept of prayer changes dramatically.

Now when Solomon had made an end of praying . . . the glory of the Lord filled the house. (2 Chr. 7:1)

When we finally stop seeking in the realization that we have everything now, the glory of Consciousness fills our hearts and minds. And to the frenzied illusions and dancing appearances of our world, Consciousness speaks the word: *Be still and know that I am God.*

And there was a great calm.

APPENDIX

30 Days of Meditations from the Lessons

Close your eyes, relax, and move gently up and into that secret place within where Reality resides, the home of Divine Consciousness. Be consciously aware of the Light of Spirit, and feel the love of the Presence in your heart center. Rest for a moment in the Silence, then open your eyes and slowly read and contemplate the meditation for the day, feeling its energy and letting the words be absorbed in consciousness. After a few minutes, return to the Silence to listen to the Word from within. Write in your journal the message you receive.

DAY 1
I do not dwell in the past, for it does not exist, and neither do any stains remain from the yesterdays of life. I have received a fresh infilling from Spirit, and all past

sorrows and compulsive fears have been removed. I am now free to climb the ladder to full and complete spiritual consciousness. I begin anew.

DAY 2

God IS. God is the one universal Presence and Power, the Cosmic Heart of Love, expressing as all that is good, true, and beautiful in life. I am that Expression.

I and the Spirit of God are one and the same. I am God being me, and God loves Itself as me.

I AM.

I AM conscious.

I AM consciously aware.

I AM consciously aware of the presence of God.

I AM consciously aware of the presence of God I AM.

I AM consciously aware of the presence of God I AM as me.

I now listen and hear the Voice of Truth speak from the stillness within.

DAY 3

I am now aware of the I mighty in the midst of me, my one Self expressing as perfect life and perfect world.

I renounce the false belief that I am a human being and accept the truth that I am pure Spirit expressing as soul and body. God is my only Being, my only Existence.

I am not a human mind, for there is only one Mind, God-Mind, and God did not create anything opposite of Itself.

I am conscious of my only Self, the Truth of my

Being. I am aware of Me, the only One, and through this awareness of my Self, the kingdom flows into perfect form and experience.

I am as Jesus—physically, mentally, emotionally, and spiritually. I am a complete being!

DAY 4

I am a spiritual being and have adapted myself to the dense energy of the earth plane, yet I was never born and I shall never die. I dismiss all such fearful ideas from my mind, and I am free to live fully now.

God's life is my life, immortal, eternal, forever.

DAY 5

I make the commitment this day to strengthen my awareness, understanding, and knowledge of God, my only Self. I shall do this by loving my Holiness with all my mind, heart, and soul. I do this now with the fullness of my being.

I acknowledge the Presence within me as the only power at work in my life and affairs. There is no other. Omnipotence, from within out, reigns supreme in my life.

DAY 6

The more I am conscious of Spirit, the more that Spirit fills my consciousness. I focus my mind on the Truth I AM and open the door, and all sense of separation dissolves as I realize my oneness with my Divine Reality. The one Light of love, peace, and understanding anchors Itself in my heart, and I feel the Divine Flame of my Holy Self illuminating my entire being.

From this moment forward, I dedicate my life to Truth. My commitment is complete, and is sustained by the will of God.

DAY 7

I have moved from karmic law to spiritual law, and Spirit is now making my decisions for me from the highest vision.

I feel dramatically different. There is a gentleness combined with an inner strength, a greater sense of peace born of love, and my life is of a higher order.

I am now a healing and harmonizing influence for everyone I encounter on my path through life.

DAY 8

Spirit, the only Power, is everywhere present. This means that my life and world are filled with harmony, loving relationships, physical wholeness, true-place success, and lavish abundance.

I have no problems. They were only false beliefs and were dissolved by Spirit flowing through me to reveal the Reality of heaven on earth.

I am aware of the activity of Spirit, the only Power at work in my consciousness. I feel the shining love, the radiating power, the flow of wisdom. I am as Jesus, and all is well.

DAY 9

I am consciously one with the Infinite Mind within, and through this awareness pulsating throughout my being, I understand Omniscience. The Spirit I AM knows all, sees my every need, and with endless love has already fulfilled that need.

In truth there is nothing to ask for. I simply have to keep my awareness on Omniscience and Its divine activity. This activity is Omnipotent, the one power pouring forth from me as a mighty fountain to reveal and express a full, complete, and joyous life. I am aware of this. I understand it. I see it. I know it.

DAY 10

I move into a New Reality now. It is my Ideal Life where everything is perfect. I turn within and see and know and feel the Ideal Body of pure energy—whole, radiant, and filled with the one Life of Spirit. I live the Body-Ideal.

DAY 11

I live and move and have my being in lavish abundance, for that is what God is. The Universal Consciousness of Abundance is individualized as me, and I see only from the highest vision the wholeness and completeness of my financial affairs. I live the Abundance-Ideal.

DAY 12

I see my ideal of perfect creative success, and in the spirit of Have, I know that what I see I shall become. I am the fullness of perfect achievement, of total victory and triumph. I do what I love and love what I do. I live the Success-Ideal.

DAY 13

My relationships are perfect, for I am loving and loved, and I see myself as everyone. I give to all the happiness and harmony that I AM and HAVE, which is overflowing and unending. I live the Relationship-Ideal.

Every other detail in my life is perfect, for I live the Ideal Life. This is now my Reality, and I watch as my world reflects this perfection. I live the Life-Ideal.

DAY 14

I am a healing power for others, for I am omnipresent, one with all in the unity of all life. I see everyone as my Self and the power is released to reveal the reality of wholeness.

I let the Light of Spirit go before me now to prove that nothing is impossible as It establishes the force field for wholeness regardless of the situation or condition. The Divine Intention of Spirit never fails, and I am a healing influence wherever I go.

DAY 15

What is this in my body calling for attention? It is a false belief that has been projected into my physical vehicle. I know that my body does not have the power to be sick, for it has no mind of its own. It is simply partaking of misqualified energy, which is giving the appearance of a malady.

I now turn within to my only Self, the I that I AM, and rest in the assurance that Omniscience and Omnipotence are maintaining my body in perfect wholeness. I connect my gaze to the all-knowing

Presence, the one Power, and let the shining Light of Love move through my mental and emotional systems, dissolving false beliefs and healing the error patterns that I have created.

I see only the Ideal Body.

DAY 16

I am the Spirit of God I AM. I am the Spirit of God I AM as lavish abundance. I am the Spirit of God I AM as lavish abundance in radiant expression in my life and affairs.

Money is a spiritual idea in my consciousness. This idea is unlimited; therefore, the expression of the idea in visible form is unlimited. I am the spiritual law governing this spiritual idea. I am the principle of abundance.

I am the radiating energy of abundance, and I let this energy fill my world and return unto me as an all-sufficiency of money and every other good thing. I am radiating the energy and love of God. I am attracting that which is mine by right of consciousness.

I no longer let my mind and emotions dwell on scarcity, for I know that no such thing exists. I place my faith in God, on the Spirit I AM, on the well of abundance that is ever flowing from the divine fountain within, and on the divine process of perfect manifestation.

DAY 17

It is God's love embodied in my consciousness that is doing the work. I relax into Mother-Substance and let love do everything for me, as me. It knows exactly what to do and is doing it now.

I do not go to God for material things. I turn within and become receptive to the flow of Mother-Love, and let my love-consciousness manifest as total fulfillment in my life.

DAY 18

I understand that the effects of this world are from the past and are not creative. One effect does not birth another, for everything emanates from consciousness.

I affirm with mind and heart that no person, place, thing, or situation in the external world has power over me, or has the power to create anew for me.

I place my total dependence on Spirit within, releasing everything to the presence of God I AM, knowing that Love has met my every need, want, or desire even before they were experienced in mind and heart.

I am as Jesus, forever one with Father-Power-Will and Mother-Substance-Love. I am a Whole Person, spiritually, mentally, emotionally, and physically—and my world reflects that Wholeness.

DAY 19

Nothing can touch me but God, for God is all there is. What is there to fear? As a Being of God, all power is within me as protective guidance, and around me as a shield of security. I place my trust in Omnipotence.

DAY 20

I see everything for the good of all, for God gives universally through omnipresence. There is neither reward nor punishment, only loving givingness con-

stantly shining as completeness, falling as nourishing wholeness for all.

What I want for me, I want for everyone.

DAY 21

It is my will that every obstacle to a whole and complete life be removed. If there is a false belief in scarcity, I decree that it be dissolved now.

If there is a lie made manifest as a physical malady, let Truth replace it now.

If an error pattern exists from judging others and is outpicturing as strained relationships, I demand that it be eliminated now. If wrong thinking has resulted in failure, it is my will that all such thoughts be corrected now.

I am ready and willing to live a rich, whole, loving, and successful life, which is my divine birthright.

God's will is mine!

DAY 22

This day I remember to reach in and touch the holy Presence in meditation, to be open to the voice of Spirit within, and to see my consciousness as the net for substance, the all-inclusive supply.

And to any undesirable experiences, I stretch forth my hand as the power of manifestation, and I radiate the energy of will to make all things new. I am as Jesus!

DAY 23

I look upon my life, my world, through spiritual eyes now, and I see only the Truth of Being. Everyone labeled man or woman is in reality the Spirit of God made visible through mind-action. Behind this physical appearance is the one radiant Self, the Christ. It is this Presence I see in every encounter. There can be no other; God is all there is.

The Truth I see in my life, my world, is Mind in perfect manifestation, whether in structure, thing, life-form, condition, or experience. Nothing that is good and beautiful is lacking, and whatever that is not of God does not exist. I see a perfect life and a perfect world, because there is nothing opposed to God and Truth has no opposite.

I know this now, and I am being lifted higher and higher in spiritual consciousness. I am as Jesus!

DAY 24

I agree to do my very best to keep my mind on the Presence I AM, to feel love and joy, to think loving thoughts toward all, and to always act from a sense of inward direction.

To accomplish this, I again release all fears, resentment, condemnation, and unforgiveness. I surrender all past mistakes and errors in judgment, and I empty out all false pride and ego-centered emotions.

Everything in my consciousness that could possibly hold me in bondage I cast upon the Christ within to be dissolved. I choose to live under grace, in spiritual consciousness. And I see and know this consciousness to be the perfect harmonizing influence in all relationships, the perfect adjustment in all situations, the perfect release from all entanglements, the perfect fulfillment in my life.

I now go forth in faith, putting my trust in Christ as my consciousness, and living each moment with a heart overflowing with gratitude, love, and joy.

DAY 25

God expressed Itself as me and I eternally live in God, with God, as the Spirit of God. The fullness of the Godhead dwells in me and expresses through me as every good and perfect thing. I am a channel for positive change in this world.

I recognize my value as an individual being living on earth at this time. As the very worthiness of God, I am part of the Grand Plan of continuing creation, and my contribution to this world is vitally important in the divine scheme of things.

Poised, powerful, and peaceful, I do my part with love and joy. I am guiltless, open and receptive to right action, and devoted to my purpose in life. Everything I do is meaningful and worthwhile. I am deserving because I know who I am.

DAY 26

I live with the relish and passion of the moment, yet I do not wander in mind from the Truth that I am a spiritual being, a single Identity ever perfect and complete.

I was not created as a separate being, for God does not know other than Itself. God is Consciousness, and it is only Consciousness that expresses individually. I am Consciousness.

I have no mind of my own, for there is only one Mind; no mortality exists, no separate beings, only the One which I am. All is Spirit.

Through love and adoration I have given myself completely to Spirit, and the awareness of Self is fading into the supreme, absolute knowing of Who I am. I live only as spiritual consciousness.

DAY 27

I honor the gifts that I have been given to see, feel, and experience that which is beyond the range of the normal. I accept this etheric vision into the subjective realm behind the physical as a heightened view of life, and simply a by-product of spiritual consciousness. I do not seek such experiences for their own sake. I let them happen as I pursue my goal of living in the highest frequencies of consciousness and being the Whole Person I was created to be.

DAY 28

I am ready to participate in the great revolution of mind and heart to reveal lasting peace on earth. As a Path Walker in this world, I am willing to join with the men and women who are coming through the dimensional passageways and offer my full cooperation. I enthusiastically consent to be a part of the team coming together from both sides of the veil to reveal the Divine Plan.

I open my imaging faculty now and see on the screen of my mind the great activity taking place through the open doors, and I let my Spirit show me the vision of the coming transformation on earth.

DAY 29

Quietly and gently, I move up to the secret place of the Most High in my consciousness. I realize my true Identity as the Christ of God, and in this Knowing, the Word is spoken through me, and the Power is loosed into the world, into the collective consciousness, and the great shift begins. Self-fulfilling prophecies are not realized, and the illusions are dispelled to reveal spiritual Reality—the one world of peace, love and joy.

The spiritual awakening is taking place through the activity of Christ. I see only peace.

DAY 30

Now I understand. That which I chase runs from me, whether health, wealth, success, or right relations. To be as Jesus means to be still and BECOME that which I seek, that which I already am and have in the completeness of my being. Then everything I desire through my vision of the ideal life will literally chase me.

I have found the point of contact within my mind that corresponds to the finished kingdom on earth, the wholeness of life where every aspiration is already fully manifest. I have seen this. I have felt it. I have walked into it in consciousness and have become it. I am all that I could conceive myself to be, and the glory of God now fills my heart and mind.

And the Word is spoken: Be still and know that I am God.

Notes

✛ ✛ ✛

INTRODUCTION
1. Kahlil Gibran, *JESUS The Son of Man* (New York: Alfred A. Knopf, Inc., 1928).

LESSON 2: Know God Aright
1. Manly P. Hall, *The Secret Teachings of All Ages: An Encyclopedic Outline of Masonic, Hermetic, Quabblistic, and Rosicrucian Symbolic Philosophy* (Los Angeles: The Philosophical Research Society, Inc., 1977), p. cxvi.
2. Newton Dillaway, ed., *The Gospel of Emerson* (Wakefield, Ma.: The Montrose Press, 1949), p. 71.
3. Alice A. Bailey, *A Treatise on Cosmic Fire* (New York: Lucis Publishing Company, 1964), p. 1136.

LESSON 3: Understand the Nature of Soul
1. Alice A. Bailey, *Letters on Occult Meditation* (New York: Lucis Publishing Company, 1966), p. 34.
2. G.R.S. Mead, *Fragments of a Faith Forgotten* (Hyde Park, NY: University Books, n.n.), p. 535.
3. Ibid, pp. 487-488.

LESSON 4: Understand Immortality
1. Michael Talbot, *The Holographic Universe* (New York: Harper-Collins Publishers, 1991), p. 161.
2. William Bramley, *The Gods of Eden* (San Jose, Ca.: Dahlin Family Press, 1989), p. 115.
3. Elaine Pagels, *The Gnostic Gospels* (New York: Vintage Books, 1981), p. 87.
4. Pagels, pp. 87, 88.

LESSON 5: Dedicate Yourself to the Spiritual Life
1. Kahlil Gibran, *JESUS The Son of Man* (New York: Alfred A. Knopf, Inc., 1928), p. 131.

LESSON 6: Rise above Karma
1. John Randolph Price, *The Angels Within Us* (New York: Fawcett Columbine/Ballantine, 1993), p. 138.

LESSON 7: Understand the Solution to Problems
1. Emmet Fox, *Power Through Constructive Thinking* (New York: Harper & Row, Publishers, 1940), pp. 178-179.

LESSON 8: Understand True Prayer
1. John Randolph Price, *With Wings As Eagles* (Carlsbad, Ca.: Hay House, Inc., 1997), pp. 76-77.

LESSON 10: Know the One Healing Presence
1. Joseph J. Weed, *Wisdom of the Mystic Masters* (West Nyack, NY: Parker Publishing Company, Inc., 1968), pp. 86-87.
2. Michael Talbot, *The Holographic Universe* (New York: Harper-Collins Publishers, 1991), p. 107.
3. Ibid, p. 103.
4. George W. Meek, ed., *Healers and the Healing Process* (Wheaton, Il.: The Theosophical Publishing House, 1977), p. 95.
5. George K. Anderson and Robert Warnock, *The World in Literature*, vol. I, Book Two (Glenview, Il.: Scott, Foresman and Company, 1959), p. 87.

6. Meek, p. 196.
7. Ibid, p. 201.

LESSON 11: Heal Thyself
1. Charles F. Haanel, *The Master Key* (Marple, Cheshire, Great Britain: Psychology Publishing Co., Ltd., 1977), pp. 212-213.

LESSON 13: Understand the Nature of Supply
1. Alice A. Bailey, *Esoteric Astrology* (New York: Lucis Publishing Company, 1951), p. 244.
2. Alice A. Bailey, *The Externalisation of the Hierarchy* (New York: Lucis Publishing Company, 1958), p. 335.
3. John Randolph Price, *A Spiritual Philosophy for the New World* (Carlsbad, Ca.: Hay House, Inc., 1997), p. 67.
4. John Randolph Price, *The Superbeings* (mass-market edition, New York: Fawcett Crest, Ballantine Books, 1988; trade edition, Carlsbad, Ca.: Hay House, Inc., 1997), p. 96.
5. Alice A. Bailey, *Esoteric Healing* (New York: Lucis Publishing Company, 1953), p. 362.

LESSON 15: Trust the Ring of Protection
1. *A Course in Miracles*, vol II, Workbook for Students (Tiburon, Ca.: Foundation for Inner Peace, 1975), p. 77.
2. Emma Curtis Hopkins, *High Mysticism* (Marina del Rey, Ca.: DeVorss & Co., Publishers, 1987), p. 32.
3. Alice A. Bailey, *Discipleship in the New Age*, vol. II (New York: Lucis Publishing Company, 1955), p. 750.

LESSON 16: See Everything for the Good of All
1. Newton Dillaway, ed., *The Gospel of Emerson* (Wakefield, Ma.: The Montrose Press, 1949), p. 69.
2. Dillaway, p. 69

LESSON 17: Understand the Will of God
1. *A Course in Miracles*, vol. I, Text (Tiburon, Ca.: Foundation for Inner Peace, 1975), pp. 149, 150.

2. Walter Starcke, *Spring '98 Letter* (Boerne, Tx.: Walter Starcke, 1998), pp. 4-5.
3. *A Course in Miracles*, vol. I, Text (Tiburon, Ca.: Foundation for Inner Peace, 1975), p. 184,

LESSON 20: Know the Dangers of Spiritual Pride
1. Alice A. Bailey, *Discipleship in the New Age*, vol. I (New York: Lucis Publishing Company, 1966), pp. 26-27.
2. John Randolph Price, *Living a Life of Joy* (New York: Fawcett Columbine/Ballantine, 1997), p. 157.
3. *A Course in Miracles*, vol. I, Text (Tiburon, Ca.: Foundation for Inner Peace, 1975), p. 167.

LESSON 21: Be Yourself
1. John Randolph Price, *Living a Life of Joy* (New York: Fawcett Columbine/Ballantine, 1997), p. 149.
2. Ibid, p. 161.

LESSON 22: Live Only As Spiritual Consciousness
1. *A Course in Miracles*, vol. II, Workbook for Students (Tiburon, Ca.: Foundation for Inner Peace, 1975), p. 171.
2. Ibid, p. 354.

LESSON 23: See the Paranormal As Normal
1. By the Editors of Time-Life Books, *Mysteries of the Unknown— Visions and Prophecies* (Alexandria, Va.: Time-Life Books, 1988), p. 9.
2. *A Course in Miracles*, vol. III, Manual for Teachers (Tiburon, Ca.: Foundation for Inner Peace, 1975), p. 59.

LESSON 24: See No Separation Between Planes of Existence
1. Jan Price, *The Other Side of Death* (New York: Fawcett Columbine/Ballantine, 1996), p. 85.
2. Ibid, pp. 107-108
3. John Randolph Price, *Angel Energy* (New York: Fawcett Columbine/Balantine, 1995), p. 187.

4. Ibid, pp. 191-192.

5. Bill Guggenheim and Judy Guggenheim, *Hello from Heaven* (Longwood, Fl.: The ADC Project, 1995), pp, 87-88.

6. James F. Twyman, *Emissary of Light* (Santa Rosa, Ca.: Aslan Publishing, 1996), pp. 219, 223.

About the Author

John Randolph Price is an internationally known award-winning author and lecturer. Formerly a CEO in the corporate world, he has devoted over a quarter of a century to researching the mysteries of ancient wisdom and incorporating those findings in the writing of many books.

In 1981, he and his wife, Jan, formed The Quartus Foundation, a spiritual research and communications organization now headquartered in the Texas hill country town of Boerne, near San Antonio.

For information about workshops, the annual Mystery School conducted by John and Jan Price, and their monthly publications, please contact:

The Quartus Foundation
P.O. Box 1768
Boerne, TX 78006
(830) 249-3985 • (830) 249-3318 (fax)
E-mail: quartus@texas.net.
The Quartus Website is: www.quartus.org

We hope you enjoyed this Hay House book.
If you would like to receive a free catalog featuring additional
Hay House books and products, or if you would like infor-
mation about the Hay Foundation, please contact:

Hay House, Inc.
P.O. Box 5100
Carlsbad, CA 92018-5100

(760) 431-7695 or **(800) 654-5126**
(760) 431-6948 (fax) or **(800) 650-5115 (fax)**

Please visit the Hay House Website at: **www.hayhouse.com**